D1109739

GEEK PARENTING

WHAT JOFFREY, JOR-EL, MALEFICENT, AND THE MCFLYS TEACH US ABOUT RAISING A FAMILY

~~~~~~~~~~

STEPHEN H. SEGAL AND VALYA DUDYCZ LUPESCU

ILLUSTRATIONS BY GREG CHRISTMAN

QUIRK BOOKS
PHILADELPHIA

Library of Congress Cataloging in Publication Number: 2015946939

ISBN: 978-1-59474-870-7

Printed in China
Typeset in Cubano, Verlag, and Bembo

Designed by Timothy O'Donnell
Cover photography: SergiyN/Shutterstock.com (boy); Tetra Images (girl)
Cover and interior illustrations by Greg Christman
Production management by John J. McGurk

Quirk Books
215 Church Street
Philadelphia, PA 19106
quirkbooks.com

10 9 8 7 6 5 4 3 2 1

TABLE OF CONTENTS

INTRODUCTION

L ittle Kal-El, rocketing toward a new family on Earth as the world of his birth explodes behind him. Sarah Connor, haunted by the knowledge that her son must someday lead his people through a terrifying robotic future. Brave Gretel, facing the life-changing decision to grab her brother Hansel's hand and escape from a kindly stranger whose gingerbread invitation has turned deadly.

Stories like these are gifts—and among the riches they give are examples that help make sense of the crazy world we live in. Hence this book, *Geek Parenting*, in which we seek wisdom, life lessons, and some much-needed humor from the parents and parental figures of geek culture's most famous fictional characters.

Parenting is hard. It may not be "stop the supervillain and save the entire universe from destruction" hard. But it weighs just as heavy on our shoulders. Parenting is what brings us to self-help guides and propels us into conversations with other moms, dads, and guardians. Beyond advice about diaper brands and prom protocol, what are we looking for when we ask these questions? To know we're not alone. To be reassured that we're not the only ones afraid of screwing up our kids. To be reminded that even Wonder Woman's mom made mistakes sometimes.

When trying to cope with the challenges of parenthood, we geeks and nerds have one advantage over other parents: an archive of fantastic stories about first contacts, epic battles, provocative ideas, and poignant sacrifices. Whether on the page, on the screen, in four-color drawings, or around a gaming table, these sagas have made us the people we are. And they will make us the parents we want to be.

The thing that parents understand, from *Battlestar Galactica*'s Commander Adama to Spider-Man's Aunt May, is that even when the world is crumbling around us—whether that means the loss of a loved one or a massive Cylon attack on the Twelve Colonies—we still have these small people entrusted into our care. Not only do we need to shield them from laser fire, but we also have to help them learn to navigate the chaos. Like the wisest wizard or ablest captain, we try to teach them to keep their light shining bright. To fine-tune their reason and creativity, protect their Achilles' heels, and master their strengths for whatever quest or trek lies ahead.

The parents in these stories live complex, tumultuous lives—on spaceships and doomed planets, in haunted houses and dark magical forests. Yet they find ways to love and care for their kids. They know that we can't abandon the task of preparing our children to face the Big Bads of the world. Not if the universe is falling apart, not if cosmic duties and magical destinies demand our time and attention. We have no choice. It is among today's kids that tomorrow's heroes will be found.

A GEEK PARENT'S PERSPECTIVE

VALYA SAYS: I think about this responsibility all the time because of my youngest daughter, who is gloriously terrifying in all her strength and stubbornness: first we help our kids to discover their power, then we teach them to use it for good. I think that's one of the most important lessons. We all find our own ways to say it, to teach it. But it all comes down to Stan Lee's famous paraphrase of Voltaire: with great power comes great responsibility. Sometimes we can teach our children that lesson by holding their hands. Other times, we need to summon the courage to step aside and allow them to make their own mistakes.

The family relationships I found waiting for me amid the stories of geek culture—superhero comics, sci-fi adventures, ancient Greek myths—have all become part of my "toolbox" as a parent. They give us models for how to teach compassion and discipline, strategies for dealing with heartbreaking decisions, ways to approach impossible situations and have hard conversations. Occasionally these characters show us how *not* to parent, like Coraline's Other Mother. That helps, too. As a parent, you need as many points of reference as you can find.

Because when you're a sleep-deprived mother of three living

in an unfamiliar city with few family or friends nearby to help, you really do feel a little bit like an alien, and you take comfort in the tales of parents who have survived the destruction of their planet, or mothers who have taken on armies or hidden their children in strange worlds to protect them.

When your nine-year-old comes home upset that a classmate is being picked on, and she doesn't know if she should risk getting bullied too by standing up for her friend, how can you not draw lessons from all the superheroes and fictional champions who fight for what is right? Sometimes being a good geek parent means talking with them; sometimes it's knowing when to watch the right movie with your kid, or share the right comic book, to help them glean the wisdom on their own.

A GEEK KID'S PERSPECTIVE

STEPHEN SAYS: My mom and dad are each a unique flavor of colorful, brainy weirdo. As a kid, I always loved that; I can't remember a time when I wasn't quietly delighted that my parents were the most interesting ones I knew.

Mom, a bookworm who grew up to be a bodybuilding champion, found early inspiration in the classic American comic book heroes. It was her enthusiasm that focused my young TV-watching habits on shows like *Batman*, *The Adventures of Superman*, *Wonder Woman*, and *The Incredible Hulk*. Dad, a briefcase-carrying bank executive with an earring, a Harley, and a shelf full of golden age science-fiction novels, plugged me into Isaac Asimov's robot stories, J. R. R.

Tolkien, *Doctor Who*, and far-out fantastical artists and musicians like M. C. Escher and Laurie Anderson. The two sets of influences met nightly after dinner, since our family meals together frequently segued straight into the 7 p.m. rerun of *Star Trek*.

In retrospect, I see that whether they'd consciously meant it this way, Dad was giving me lots of exciting stories of imaginative thinkers who figured out creative solutions to the universe's problems, while Mom was giving me lots of exciting stories of morally brave outsiders who cared enough about their weaker neighbors to stand up against those who would harm them. The result was that, without ever getting dry lectures on any of these serious topics, I spent my childhood gradually developing the idea that the awesomest thing I could possibly be was a kind, smart, unique person who tried to make a difference in the world. Like Frodo Baggins. Or Lois and Clark. Or the Doctor.

AND SO . . .

Ray Bradbury once wrote that science fiction is the "most important literature in the history of the world, because it's the history of ideas, the history of our civilization birthing itself." What better way to draw parenting wisdom than by dipping into the creative continuum that encourages humanity to dream big, reach for the stars, and imagine societies of peace and equality?

We, your authors, are not child psychologists. We're just two high-functioning nerds who've long charted our lives, and our families' lives, by the never-ending fount of practical and useful geek wisdom we've encountered in the pop and not-so-pop culture that helped shape us into the adults we are today. In this book we set out to comb through geek culture, family by family—magical families, outer-space families, futuristic families, and superhero families—looking for as many moments of clarity and inspiration as we could find.

Not only did we become better acquainted with some unexpected depths in the favorite characters we grew up with—*Trek*'s Benjamin and Jake Sisko; *The Addams Family*'s Morticia, Gomez, and clan—we also discovered several amazingly inspirational new stories we hadn't experienced. That's the other use of this book we hope you'll share: a guide to expanding your bookshelf and your video queue, as well as a guide to some of the epic, cosmic questions that are likely to present themselves during your journey through parenthood.

Leonard Nimoy, one of the brightest beacons of geek wisdom and compassion, passed away while we were writing this book. His iconic Spock is best known for the benediction "Live long and prosper." We hope you will do that very thing, and we'd like to launch you into *Geek Parenting* with another of his quotes: "There are always possibilities."

As we wake each day, ready or not to deal with whatever challenges may be involved with this planetary rotation cycle, that's the core truth we try to hold on to. The future is never set in stone, and every young life marks a newer, fresher attempt at making sense of this mad, infinite universe we're all a part of. And when you get right down to it, isn't that really what having kids is all about?

1

~~~~~~~~~~

THERE'S NO PLACE LIKE HOME*

Creating a local environment conducive to
the development of nascent life forms.

* Dorothy Gale, *The Wizard of Oz*

TAKE A BREAK FROM FIGHTING OFF BORG WARSHIPS TO PLAY BALL WHENEVER YOU CAN.

Where *Star Trek: The Next Generation* promised us a look at family life on board a Starfleet vessel, it was left to the follow-up series *Deep Space Nine* to actually deliver. Commander Benjamin Sisko and his son Jake might just represent the strongest, fullest, deepest father–son relationship ever depicted in onscreen science fiction—and, indeed, one of the richest ever seen on television.

The very first scene of the show's very first episode shows the space battle in which Jake's mother is killed. It's an immediate grounding in the family-first soul of a father and husband to whom love is everything. As *Deep Space Nine* unfolds over the next seven seasons, the Siskos' relationship is never hobbled by the sort of gimmicky plot points that *Next Generation* writers stuck Beverly and Wesley Crusher with ("Hey, Mom, I invented a gadget that could destroy the ship!"). Ben and Jake are allowed simply to be a working dad and his son living on a space station, and that is a beautiful thing.

Nowhere is this point better illustrated than in the pair's love of baseball. The Siskos work in outer space, but they're from New Orleans, the town where Shoeless Joe Jackson led the Pelicans to a pennant in 1910, and where Dazzy Vance struck out 163 batters in 1921. For Commander Sisko, tossing around a ball and collecting good old-fashioned trading cards with his son brings mellow relaxation amid the stress of trying to keep peace between alien races inclined to kill one another. Although the series focuses on the Bajoran-Cardassian-Dominion conflicts, the Ben-and-Jake moments that resonate are more personal: the baseball game they play against the crew of a Vulcan starship, or the passion for writing fiction that Jake inherits from his dad.

Theirs is an example we can all stand to follow. So many of us, whether single parents or committed couples, are working harder and longer to pay the bills. It's maddeningly easy for any adult to get caught up in job demands, especially when these pressures start early in the morning and continue till bedtime. Benjamin Sisko, Starfleet's greatest dad, reminds us that as important as the work is, there is something we're doing it all *for*. The precious moments when we enjoy our children's company are that something.

EVEN IMMORTAL GODS HAVE THE URGE TO PUNCH THEIR SMARTASS SIBLINGS IN THE FACE.

Oh, Loki. It always has to be about you, doesn't it? When Thor celebrates his eighteen-thousandth birthday (or whatever), and Odin cheers the future king's coming of age, you have to cry *"But I-I-I-I'd be a better king!"* When frost giants want to murder your dad and enslave your neighbors, you have to be all *"That'll show those losers they should have been nice to me."* When a nice old German man tells you that your power-mad rule-the-world spiel ain't really impressing the grown-ups because Hitler did it first (and better), you just gotta come back with *"Nuh-uh, I am a special snowflake and it is you who are the one who sucks."*

But then again . . . Thor, is the smugness really necessary? Aren't the massive biceps and piercing blue eyes enough? Have you tried, perhaps, *not* being Asgard's arrogant star quarterback? For the umpteenth time, yes, we see how good you are with your hammer. Can you really *not* let your brother have a turn with it? He's littler, you know. He looks up to you.

We always want our kids to be one another's best friends—to love and support and be there for each other, no matter what. But nowhere is the difference between family and friends more starkly on display than in the relationships between siblings. Brothers and sisters are peers; they enjoy a common upbringing and history; they share genetic programming. Yet thanks to the way the chromosome tumbles, they're also prone to being wildly different individuals with utterly unmatched personalities. Sometimes they are friends. Other times, they're more like civil roommates trying to make the best out of having been produced by the same parents.

Even if siblings do like each other, it's still a challenge to wait for someone else to get the heck out of the bathroom every single day for some eighteen years straight. So when you're breaking up their third fight of the afternoon, take comfort in knowing that all the contention is perfectly normal. Even in our greatest myths, films, and comics, siblings don't always get along.

Jessica Hamby and Bill Compton teach us:

WHEN YOUR COFFIN IS UNDER MY ROOF, YOU HAVE TO FOLLOW MY RULES.

n *True Blood*, the late 2000s television series based on novelist Charlaine Harris's Southern Vampire Mysteries, the strongest examples of kinship are those forged by blood: the blood of vampires and their progeny. The bond between them is sacred. Once "makers" carefully choose their offspring, they are responsible for the care and well-being of the "baby-vampire." Bill Compton isn't looking to have a daughter, let alone a teenager, when he's ordered by the vampire Magister to turn seventeen-year-old Jessica Hamby into a vampire. In fact, in his 140 undead years, Bill has not made a single vampire. Because Bill believes vampirism to be a curse, he even denies his birth daughter on her deathbed when she begs him to turn her. With Jessica, Bill has no choice: becoming a maker is his punishment for killing one of his kind.

It's a maker's responsibility to indoctrinate the new vampire into the rules of vampire society, teach them how to take care of their new bodies and feed responsibly. Coming from an ultraconservative and abusive background in her past life, Jessica isn't looking for a new father. She is eager to embrace both her freedom and her vampire nature. Like any teenager, Jessica wants to explore and experiment, to discover whom and what she likes. Meanwhile, as far as parenting goes, Bill is drawing upon practices and principles from the last time he was a father—in the middle of the nineteenth century. In many ways, the pair is like any other parent and teenager: she's testing out her independence, he's trying to establish rules, and hopefully no one gets killed in the process. "Your bedtime will be at 4 a.m. and not a minute later," Bill says to Jessica when she comes to stay with him. "And whilst you're under my roof, hunting is completely forbidden." The details may be different, but the idea is the same everywhere—children, especially teens, need house rules.

Our kids may not have to worry about deadly stakes and holy water, but in their world they may encounter plenty of other hazards, from peer pressure and online predators to drugs and alcohol. Yet they feel invincible, think they know everything, and believe they are ready for whatever comes their way. We have them in our care for only a short time (a little longer if we're vampires). A give-and-take over things like curfews and driving privileges occurs as our kids near adulthood. It requires clear and consistent rules, the background against which negotiations take place. Put another way: it is rules that keep our kids safe and give them the chance to prove themselves, too.

Nobody and Mr. and Mrs. Owens teach us:

GET TO KNOW YOUR NEIGHBORS, HOWEVER DARK AND STORMY THE NEIGHBORHOOD MIGHT SEEM.

After his family is murdered, the toddler in Neil Gaiman's 2008 fantasy novel *The Graveyard Book* is taken in and cared for by the supernatural occupants of the cemetery across the street. The ghosts of Mr. and Mrs. Owens become the boy's adoptive parents. And Nobody, as they name him— or "Bod," for short—is granted the Freedom of the Graveyard, allowing him certain privileges that include the ability to move through solid objects and communicate with all the ghostly residents. Bod's childhood, although unconventional, is loving and happy.

No parent can do everything. Gaps will need to be filled by other people. Bod's cemetery is populated by ancient ghosts, witches, Hounds of God, and other entities. Mr. and Mrs. Owens give him a home and love, but Bod needs someone corporeal to provide for his physical needs. The graveyard's caretaker, Silas, becomes his mentor and guardian, caring for him in ways that the Owenses cannot. Silas also calls in the services of Miss Lupescu, who teaches Bod valuable lessons in language and lore and saves his life on more than one occasion. As Bod says: "I learned about ghoul-gates. I learned to Dreamwalk. Miss Lupescu taught me how to watch the stars. Silas taught me silence. I can Haunt. I can Fade. I know every inch of this graveyard." Sooner or later, each one of Bod's ghostly neighbors plays a part in preparing him to be a well-rounded and thoughtful young man.

In the modern world, it is rarer than perhaps it once was to be closely tied to the people who live around us. We may live our lives behind fences, both literal and metaphoric, but there's something to be gained by turning nearby strangers into real neighbors. The greatest neighbor of them all, Fred Rogers, once said: "We live in a world in which we need to share responsibility. It's easy to say, 'It's not my child, not my community, not my world, not my problem.' Then there are those who see the need and respond. I consider those people my heroes."

Bod is lucky to have these kinds of heroes in his own backyard, which in this case happens to be a graveyard. He finds neighbors who'll take the time to chat with him, offer advice, and teach him things. *The Graveyard Book* shows us the benefit of raising a child within a community—even if that community isn't a conventional one.

BE AN AVATAR OF THE PRINCIPLES YOU WANT YOUR CHILD TO LEARN.

A valuable lesson to learn early on is that not everything in life comes easily. There are arenas in which our children excel, and places where they struggle. They may do everything possible to avoid an activity they find challenging—be it public speaking or algebra, foreign languages or gymnastics. But we can't go through life performing only the tasks that come easy to us.

In the animated TV show *The Legend of Korra,* even the reincarnated peacemaker of the world, with her hundreds of lifetimes of experience, has strengths and weaknesses. Korra, the most recent incarnation of the Avatar, is able to manipulate, or "bend," the mystic elements of fire, earth, and water. But her hotheadedness keeps Korra from the calm state of mind needed to manipulate the element of air.

To maintain peace, which is her duty as Avatar, Korra must master all four elements. And so she turns to the oldest living air-bending master, Tenzin—son of the previous Avatar—for training. The impulsive Korra finds it difficult to learn from the stoic guru, whom she tells: "Believe me, I'd be happy to find another air-bending master, but you're the only one. We're stuck with each other." She contemplates quitting, because up to that point everything else she's tried has come relatively easy to her. But the patient Tenzin continues to stand by and challenges her to keep trying. As her mentor, he not only teaches her the techniques she must learn, but he also provides her with a living example of how an air-bender must behave.

From Tenzin we learn that the best way to teach our children anything is by modeling the behavior we wish them to emulate. It's a variation on the maxim "Be the change you wish to see in the world." We must show patience to impart patience; we teach kindness by being kind. True, we're only human. None of us can be avatars of virtue at all times. What's important is that we try to live up to our values—and keep trying even when inevitably we fall short. By demonstrating our own perseverance, we encourage our children also to persevere. After all, how can we expect them to put forth an effort that we refuse to make ourselves?

Lydia, Charles, and Delia Deetz teach us:

DANCE, DANCE, DANCE, SEÑORA.

When Lydia Deetz, teen hero of the 1988 film *Beetlejuice,* moves into the rickety house haunted by the ghosts of Adam and Barbara Maitland, she's a brooding goth girl with a flashy artist stepmother and a frazzled, recovering-workaholic father. Typical of most teenagers, she feels alienated and misunderstood. Lydia meets Adam and Barbara, specters unwilling to share their space with the dysfunctional new family. Lydia's parents ignore the haunting and dismiss her concerns as part of a quirky teen rebellion.

Even the most tuned-in parents can accidentally trigger adolescent sulkiness; *Beetlejuice* adds ornery ghosts to the mix. The domestic dysfunction comes to a head when Lydia's stepmother throws a dinner party, and the angst-ridden girl is left glaring over the fine china at her parents' glib, pretentious New York friends. Enter Lydia's new ghost pals, whose unconventional haunting techniques include a supernatural calypso number. Not only does the interruption finally get Lydia's parents' attention, it completely changes the uptight mood.

There's something to be said for spontaneous dance breaks. Sometimes the only way to stop the cycle of cranky sibling squabbling or homework-related whining is to put on some Harry Belafonte hits, or whatever tunes are cued up in your playlist, and get a groove on. After a song or two, even the most determined scowler has likely cracked a smile, or at least taken a few mental steps outside the downward emotional spiral of the earlier crisis. Indeed, a spur-of-the-moment dance party is an excellent method for renewing everyone's energy to conquer the next task at hand—be it algebra or Betelgeuse.

Spock, Sarek, and Amanda teach us:

INHERITING DAD'S POINTED EARS DOESN'T MEAN A KID IS JUST LIKE DAD. THAT IS ILLOGICAL.

pock is a Vulcan. That's clearly his single most defining trait, right? He's brilliant, he's dispassionate, he's a coolly calculating strategist from a planet of stoic intellectuals. And, of course, he's got those devilishly sharp otherworldly features: the angular-tipped ears, the wicked cheekbones, the up-slashing eyebrows. He's practically the spitting image of his father, Sarek, the galactically renowned ambassador who represents Vulcan to the entire United Federation of Planets. As his shipmate Dr. McCoy never tires of pointing out, Spock is a cold-hearted, green-blooded alien who harbors the soul of a computer.

There's just one problem with all the obvious assumptions about Spock—they're wrong. Or, rather, they're woefully insufficient for describing who Spock really is, as we see again and again over the course of the classic *Star Trek*'s seventy-nine TV episodes and six movies. Spock's imperturbably rational Vulcan facade is the result of a struggle he's been fighting since childhood. It's his attempt to do his father, and his people, proud in the face of a reality Spock is embarrassed to admit: he's really his mother's son. When push comes to shove—when innocent lives are at stake, when truth and beauty are threatened, when his friends Kirk and McCoy are in danger—

Spock's core self emerges. He's soulful. He's sensitive. He sees life not merely as a math equation but as a sacred experience. As Kirk says: "Of all the souls I encountered in my travels, his was the most . . . human."

His father expected Spock to be a Vulcan, so that's the persona Spock cultivated. As a result, Spock doesn't find true contentment and inner peace until well into middle adulthood, after his traumatic encounter with the sentient entity known as V'Ger. While recovering, Spock comes to terms with the truth that his mother's emotional heritage is just as central to his being as his father's more analytical legacy.

As parents, it's easy for us to unthinkingly assume that a child who has traits A and B in common with one parent must share traits C, D, and E as well. Spock's experience shows that as a fallacy to beware of. If not corrected, it's a delusion which can set up false expectations that even Vulcan-caliber logic might never be able to dislodge.

Lord Eddard Stark and the Stark children teach us:

A DIREWOLF IS A STARK'S BEST FRIEND.

When six orphaned direwolf cubs are found in the Wolfswood beside their dead mother, Lord Eddard Stark allows each of his children to have one. The ancient wolves are the sigil for House Stark, and their appearance North of the Wall is auspicious. Even the bastard Jon Snow gets the albino runt of the litter. The six cubs—Grey Wind, Lady, Nymeria, Summer, Shaggy Dog, and Ghost—quickly bond with their respective new masters, and before long it's impossible to imagine the events of *Game of Thrones* without them. What starts out as the rescue of six orphaned pups becomes a lifelong relationship for most of the Stark children.

And so it goes with pets. They provide children with unconditional love over the course of their lives. Friends and enemies come and go, kings are replaced on the iron throne, but a beloved pet is loyal till the end. However, choosing to adopt an animal is a decision not to be entered into lightly. As Eddard Stark stresses to his children, *they* will be responsible for caring for the direwolves in life and in death. It's important for children to understand just what will be expected of them if they want to bring a pet into the home. A family must have the resources and the space to accommodate another living creature with needs and desires. Yards are good for dogs, apartments are suitable for cats, vast acres of forest around a castle are what make a direwolf happy.

It's a lot to consider, but the impact of a family pet can be so powerful it's worth consideration. Having an animal companion is an excellent way to teach children important life skills and compassion. They learn how to care for living creatures who are dependent upon them for their health and happiness in the form of food, cleanliness, exercise, training, and veterinary visits. In return, children gain a best friend who will stand by them when other friends are fickle or battles are fought over land and loyalty. These lessons are valuable for anyone, whether they rule the North or just lay claim to the top bunk in their bedroom.

The Grandson and the Grandfather teach us:

READ TO THEM.

When William Goldman wrote *The Princess Bride: S. Morgenstern's Classic Tale of True Love and High Adventure* in 1973, Atari was still developing its game system. By the time Rob Reiner made the film based on the book, in 1987, Nintendo had surpassed ColecoVision and Atari as the leading game console. Video games were competing with television for kids' attention, and critics were grumbling about an age of postliteracy. Which makes it notable that the *Princess Bride* film opens with a boy who is sick in bed, playing Atari. His mother announces a visit from his grandfather, whose gift of an old hardcover storybook is met with skepticism. "When I was your age, television was called books," the grandfather explains. "And this is a special book. It was the book my father used to read to me when I was sick, and I used to read it to your father, and today, I'm gonna read it to you."

The grandson listens reluctantly to the story only after his grandfather promises him an adventure to rival any video game: "Fencing. Fighting. Torture. Revenge. Giants. Monsters. Chases. Escapes. True love. Miracles." After a few initial groans and protests, the boy is sucked into the story, interjecting questions and growing emotionally invested in the characters. By the time brave Westley and his comrades reach the Pit of Despair, the boy has been completely won over—he has discovered the joy of reading.

Today's kids have more forms of entertainment competing for their time and attention than ever before. But as we and our WiFi-enabled progeny geek out over the latest apps, games, and media streams, let's not forget the unique appeal of reading a story aloud to our kids. We can pick up the pace, slow it down, or hit pause, depending on their interest. We can revisit favorite parts again and again. We can heighten the suspense or skip over passages that might be too scary. We can create our own character voices and encourage them to join in. We can even change the tale if we want to, asking our audience to guess what happens next. No other platform offers as much interactivity. All we need for this multimedia experience is a book and some light to read by. No cables, Internet connection, Bluetooth speakers, downloads, or wireless routers required.

Makeda, Abby, and their Celestial family teach us:

DON'T PLAY FAVORITES, OR YOUR KIDS MAY LOSE THEIR MOJO.

Makeda and Abby are the daughters of a demigod in Nalo Hopkinson's remarkable 2013 book *Sister Mine*. Born conjoined, the twins are separated in an operation that leaves Abby missing part of her leg and Makeda without her magical mojo. While Abby is cherished for her beautiful voice by her father's Celestial family, Makeda seems to lack any magical gifts. Makeda feels inadequate and unremarkable, and her family's adoration of Abby only makes it worse.

It's natural for children to measure themselves against their siblings. But for parents of multiple children, the challenge is finding ways to celebrate the unique accomplishments of each child while resisting the urge to compare those triumphs. Comments like "Your brother gets straight As every year" or "Your sister made the soccer team on her first tryout" pit siblings against one another. The last thing we want is for our children to feel they're competing for our love or attention.

Makeda seems not to have any of the magical ability her family prizes, but she does have facets to her personality that are underestimated by those around her. For instance, she's an amazing cook, making her sister delicacies like stewed guinea hen and manioc with batata dumplings. Indeed, for all that she is taken for granted, Makeda spends most of her life serving as her twin's primary support system. Perhaps even more important, her mortal weaknesses force her to be ingenious and brave in facing down magical threats. Makeda's story is a potent reminder what can happen if we focus on what our children lack, instead of taking note of the gifts they possess. Not only do we sow the seeds of sibling rivalry, but we're also likely to miss the very things that make them extraordinary.

YOU HAVE A MAGIC BAG OF TRICKS . . . USE IT!

I n one of the most iconic scenes in Disney's 1964 film *Mary Poppins*, the Banks siblings watch in amazement as their magical new nanny calmly lifts out of her handbag a succession of objects that couldn't possibly fit inside: a hat stand, a lamp, a potted plant. "Never judge things by their appearance—even carpetbags," she tells them. Mary Poppins, world's most supercalifragilisticexpialidocious childcare professional, stands ready to provide her charges with whatever they may need, whether tool, story, or adventure.

It sure would be nice to have one of those bottomless bags . . . Well, rest assured—every parent does, metaphorically at least. Granted, most of us are neither as flawlessly appointed as Julie Andrews's Mary Poppins, nor as cosmic as the version we meet in P. L. Travers's original books (which, among other things, whisks the Banks children off to talk with sea creatures and dance with planets).

We may not be able to take our kids for a picnic under the ocean, but we can take them for a walk when they're feeling stir-crazy and talk about what we see along the way. We can tell them about a sad moment from our own childhood when they're lonely. We can look at old family photos when they're bored or take them to visit a favorite relative (even if he doesn't float around the room when he laughs).

Walt Whitman writes in his poem "Song of Myself": "I am large, I contain multitudes." So does everybody! We are all collections of life experiences distinctive to each of us, and we can use that knowledge to engage our kids, from childhood explorations and teenage experiments to adventures in love and heartache. Much like Mary Poppins's carpetbag (or Doctor Who's TARDIS), people are bigger on the inside. We're full of stories that can transport our children to times and places from our past, from our imagination, from our hopes and our dreams. There are always more wonders we can share, if we reach for them when we need them.

Donnie, Samantha, and Rose Darko teach us:

ALWAYS QUESTION YOUR COMMITMENT TO SPARKLE MOTION.

What *is* Sparkle Motion? Is it an enthusiastic group of young girls looking to fulfill their dancing dreams? Is it the ambition of an overinvolved dance-mom coach? Or is it something else entirely, something emblematic of the overscheduled and helicopter style of parenting so prevalent today? In the weird and wonder-filled universe of the 2001 film *Donnie Darko*, Sparkle Motion is all these things at once.

Parents are invited to participate in so many areas of kids' lives: classrooms, sports teams, play dates, after-school clubs . . . It's easy to stretch our kids and ourselves too thin. Sparkle Motion encapsulates all those time-sucking activities. It's everything we're told we should care about—but really don't.

"Sometimes I question your commitment to Sparkle Motion," dance coach Kitty Farmer tells Rose Darko.Kitty's guilt trip works, and Rose agrees to chaperone the girls' dance group when they travel to Los Angeles. Later, the plane carrying Rose and Samantha and the girls will be the same one to have its engine fall out and crash through the Darkos' roof. Overscheduling rarely leads to such tragic consequences. But a more common type of crash—exhaustion—seldom leads to happy kids *or* happy parents.

Papa Smurf and his Smurfs smurf us:

WHETHER YOU'RE THREE APPLES HIGH OR THREE FEET TALL, RESPECT YOUR ELDERS.

The oldest among the baby-boom generation have reached retirement age, and more of the cohort are joining their ranks every year. The result: more elders are living among us than ever before.

The Smurfs first appeared in Belgian comics in 1958; in the 1980s, they got their own Saturday morning cartoon. Since the beginning, Papa Smurf has been leading and caring for all of his "little Smurfs," who turn to him for advice and magical assistance. In turn, Papa shows deference to his elders when Grandpa Smurf returns to the village after having left Papa alone as a Smurfling to set out on a globe-spanning quest.

There was a time when, like Papa Smurf, elders held an honored place as teachers and leaders respected for their life experiences. Today, it's easy to miss out on the insights offered by our Mama and Papa Smurfs. Kids learn by example, so if they see us appreciating our parents, grandparents, and trusted older adults, then they'll get the message that these folks are valuable. Our children can learn from their wisdom, seniors receive the attention and respect they deserve, and we pave the road for the not-so-distant future when we take our place as the next generation of elders. That's not a bad outcome for emulating a bunch of tiny blue forest creatures.

Lettie, Ginnie, and Gran Hempstock teach us:

THERE'S A REASON IT'S CALLED COMFORT FOOD.

When the narrator in Neil Gaiman's 2013 book *The Ocean at the End of the Lane* is seven years old, the suicide of his family's lodger sets off a chain of events that culminates in a harrowing attack on the narrator's world. Throughout it all, one constant remains: the support of the three generations of Hempstock women. Lettie, Ginnie, and Gran keep him safe; their home is his sanctuary, and their food nourishes his body and spirit. That begins when they serve him porridge with blackberry jam. "I swished it around with my spoon before I ate it," he recalls, "swirling it into a purple mess, and was as happy as I have ever been about anything. It tasted perfect." It's the first of many instances when delicious food is prepared and served by the Hempstocks—a smorgasbord of consolation in the form of pancakes with plum jam, spotted dick with custard, fresh honeycomb with cream, beef and roast potatoes, and more delectable dishes.

Food can make witches and time travelers of us all. The taste of a family recipe transports us back to a pivotal moment in our lives. The smell of a favorite meal evokes happy memories from simpler times. It can remind us of a beloved person or place long gone. Food has the power of nostalgia and connection—and we frequently turn that power outward to offer love to others. When someone is sick, we bring hearty soups or stews to strengthen their bodies. When someone is grieving, we deliver salads or casseroles, something easy to reheat or serve cold. In situations where we feel unsure of how to help a person stricken with tragedy, bringing a meal is a simple way to express our concern, sympathy, and desire to make things better.

We never know which of the meals we feed our kids might end up becoming deeply meaningful to them: grilled cheese on a rainy afternoon, tacos on a birthday, or peanut butter and jelly sandwiches for school lunch. But it's a good reason to indulge in their favorite foods from time to time and pay attention to the culinary traditions that arise from our family's eating habits.

Like the Hempstocks, when we feed our kids, we nourish them in myriad ways. Someday, when they're feeling sad, they may make Mom's mashed potatoes or Dad's pad thai. They'll find comfort in those dishes, remembering the love that went into their preparation and the time spent enjoying a meal either together or alone.

Connor and Angel teach us:

SOMETIMES YOU NEED
TO GIVE THEM SOME SPACE.

To say that children may get moody is a bit of an understatement. During times of tween tantrums, preteen meltdowns, or teenage surliness, a little space may be the best thing for all parties involved. That's certainly what the title character of *Angel*, the *Buffy the Vampire Slayer* spin-off series, found. A vampire cursed with a soul, Angel never thought he'd be a parent in the undead half of his existence. Especially not father to a teenager with superhuman powers and extreme anger-management issues. The son of Angel and his longtime vampire lover Darla, Connor is born when his mother sacrifices herself to save him. After a few months in his father's care, Connor is kidnapped by Angel's enemies and raised in a hell dimension to despise his father—returning as a teenager full of resentment and dreams of vengeance. Despite strides toward reconciliation, Connor seals his father in a metal box and sinks him to the bottom of the ocean. Angel is eventually rescued and confronts his son. He tells Connor that he loves him—then kicks him out of the house. Both parties need space to think about what their relationship will look like in the future.

Our kids will, at some point, get angry and need time to deal with their emotions. Giving them a chance to think before we yell back will ultimately make for a more productive conversation. Parents, too, can benefit from time to cool down and think more clearly. We can make sure that we're not just reacting to behavior, but looking deeper to find the root of the problem (like, exactly which hell dimension did our child spend too much time in? Was it the TV room?). Giving our children space also allows them the opportunity to develop coping mechanisms for anger and stress—tactics like blowing off steam with physical exercise, writing in a journal, or, in Connor's case, killing evil vampires.

Space is not the same thing as neglect. Angel is sure to look in on Connor to make sure his son is okay. It's important for kids to understand that we're still here, that the distance between us is temporary; we'll resume interaction when tempers have cooled or when they need us. That kind of space can be scary for parents because it acknowledges a key milestone: our kids have reached an age when we can no longer simply tell them what they need to do. But it's a necessary part of parenting, and an important moment of growth, for child and adult alike.

Dorothy and Auntie Em teach us:

WHATEVER KANSAS YOUR
TEEN LIVES IN, IT FEELS
LIKE A BLACK-AND-WHITE
TOWN STIFLING THEIR
TECHNICOLOR SOUL.

t's so easy, isn't it, to believe that the grass is greener on the other side? Just look at Dorothy. In the *Wizard of Oz*, she isn't a malcontent; she isn't especially overflowing with emo. She begins the story as a fairly well-adjusted, well-mannered teenager who loves her aunt, loves her uncle, and loves her dog. Even so, one miserable neighbor's bad attitude is enough to put Dorothy straight off whatever fondness she might have for her homey little Kansas county.

When Miss Gulch threatens to have Dorothy's dog euthanized, the sensitive teenager doesn't see it as a resolvable situation best addressed by rational authorities. Dorothy jumps right into declaring that she'd be better off moving somewhere else entirely—somewhere "troubles melt like lemon drops" and "the dreams that you dare to dream really do come true."

Dorothy is indulging in the same "This place sucks" reverie that adolescents generally do, no matter whether their formative home is a family farm, a coal-mining town, or a seaside resort. What she learns in Oz is that every place, no matter how magical, has an Almira Gulch or a Wicked Witch prone to dragging everyone down. By corollary, she deduces correctly that the inverse is true as well. Her Auntie Em was right: there's magic and wonder to be found even in her own ordinary backyard.

That's a hard truth to impart secondhand. It frequently takes some far-off adventuring to be able to truly see one's childhood home, one's default ambiance, for all that it is. We want our kids to appreciate where they're from. But we should keep in mind that they may need to visit other locales before they're ready to identify their place in the world.

Peter, Susan, Edmund, and Lucy Pevensie,
along with Professor Kirke, teach us:

BOREDOM CAN OPEN MAGIC DOORS TO ADVENTURE.

t is the height of World War II, and when London is barraged by bombings, the four young Pevensie siblings are sent to live with Professor Kirke in the English countryside. One rainy day, when they've grown tired of books and radio, the children go off to explore their host's enormous manor. After wandering through bedrooms and hallways, young Lucy steps inside an old wardrobe and discovers a doorway to the magical land of Narnia. So begin the adventures of C. S. Lewis's seven-volume Chronicles of Narnia series.

Now take a moment and imagine what might have happened if Peter, Susan, Edmund, and Lucy had smartphones or iPads. Would they have sat quietly in their attic, playing Minecraft until the war was over? They might never have met Aslan the noble lion or helped the Narnian army defeat the White Witch.

The Pevensie children's adventures are fictional, of course. But how many great artists, scientists, philosophers, and explorers were able to imagine the possibilities and dream big because, as children, they had the free time to do so? Boredom is creative potential. It's the luxury to daydream, to make those connections between what is real and what is possible. Boredom creates space in our busy minds where imagination can flourish. Today's portable devices put games and social media at our fingertips. These tools allow kids to inform themselves about current events and connect with other like-minded children in ways that were impossible decades ago. This is wonderful. And yet . . . are we too quick to fill our family's downtime with technology? How often do our kids stare out the window? Go for aimless walks and bike rides with friends? Make-believe?

The kind-hearted professor doesn't try to fill the Pevensie children's days with activities and lessons. He welcomes them into his world, allows them the time and space to explore, and afterward is interested in hearing about their adventures. When our kids come to us complaining that they are bored, what they're really saying is they need a little help getting started on their next daydream. Answering that call takes a bit more effort than installing a new app, but it shows that we care about how they spend their time. And maybe, once in a while, we can go along on their next adventure.

Morticia, Gomez, Wednesday, and Pugsley Addams teach us:

IF THEY'RE CREEPY AND THEY'RE KOOKY, THEN YOU'RE THE ONE WHO'S LUCKY.

With the black-and-white *Addams Family* television show that ran from 1964 to 1966, America met its most iconic family of weirdoes: the spooky but loving married couple, Morticia and Gomez Addams, and their two black-clad children, brother Pugsley and sister Wednesday. Named for their creator—the *New Yorker* cartoonist Charles Addams, who depicted the characters in a series of one-panel magazine gags starting in 1938—the Addams family lived a 24/7/365 Halloween lifestyle. They were surrounded by monstrous and ghoulish relatives and cheerfully obsessed with all death's trappings. The show's running gag was that visitors to their gothic mansion were invariably horrified by this macabre existence, whereas the ever-smiling, blithely unworried Addamses were creeped out by conventional expressions of American wholesomeness, like flowering hedges and apple pie.

Though morbid on the surface, *The Addams Family* brought

us inside the home of one of the most compassionate, altruistic clans that's ever appeared on television. Every week we saw Morticia, Gomez, and their children helping strangers, sympathizing with misunderstood monsters and oddballs, and challenging people's expectations of what a family looks like. The parents teach Wednesday and Pugsley, by example and via advice, that one can be happy without fitting into the standards set by society. That's a startlingly subversive message to find on a network TV sitcom, even today.

But it's an important one. The world is a judgmental place. Messages from the media, pressure from peers, criticism from teachers—children have a lot to sort through as they cultivate their authentic selves. Home, the Addamses teach us, should be both a sanctuary and a playground, a place where children feel safe to explore who they want to be. In the case of a child like Wednesday, that may mean headless dolls, a collection of live spiders, and occasionally shooting your big brother out of a cannon. Odd choices? Perhaps. But as long as the kids aren't hurting anyone (or themselves—and, to be fair, the Addams kids seemed more resilient than most), why not emulate Gomez and Morticia and let children joyfully explore the darkness? They may just find beauty in the unexpected.

DON'T WAIT TO BECOME THE WALKING DEAD—BE THE WALKING ALIVE. STARTING TODAY.

ife gets busy. There's always some chore that needs doing: a meal to prepare, homework to finish, a lawn to mow, an undead human to behead. Maybe that last one isn't on your to-do list as often is it is for the *Walking Dead* crowd. But if people in that comic book turned blockbuster TV show can take the time to appreciate one another in the midst of a zombie apocalypse, we should be able to carve out a few moments for an occasional heart-to-heart with our kids.

Going for a walk can be a great way to connect and communicate. For Michonne and the young Carl Grimes, many of their most honest and vulnerable moments are shared

while walking—on patrols, scavenging for supplies, or looking for the next sanctuary. Upon joining Rick Grimes's group, Michonne is resistant to connect with most people, let alone the children. Just after the outbreak, her three-year-old son Andre was killed in a zombie attack. The brutal reality of her loss transformed

Michonne into the fierce and seemingly dispassionate warrior we initially encounter. Eventually, however, she softens and forms an especially close relationship with Rick's son Carl. For Carl, whose mother has died, Michonne serves as a female authority figure and emotional caretaker. Carl is the only person in whom Michonne confides about her deceased son. In a reality fraught with danger, they each have the other's back.

Even when we're not dodging zombies, taking a walk removes many of the distractions competing for our attention. A family amble around the neighborhood or through the park gets us out of our heads and into the world. Precocious toddlers and young children love the chance to ask questions while meandering. If you're unsure how to start a conversation with a grumbly tween or a reluctant preteen, point out a car that reminds you of when you learned to drive, or a dog on a walk that looks like a former pet. Perhaps more important, ask questions of them: Who do you think lives in that house? Can you see a face in that tree? What kind of an apartment would you like to live in when you're older? Whatever we see, whatever we talk about, wherever we go, remember that when we set out on a stroll, we are spending time together, come what may.

Coraline and the Other Mother teach us:

YOU MAY PICTURE THE PERFECT PARENTS IN YOUR MIND'S EYE— BUT THERE'S NO SUCH THING.

Many of the classic fairy tales we've grown up with—Snow White, Cinderella, Hansel and Gretel—begin with the absence of the heroine's deceased mother, a void into which a sinister anti-mother steps. Coraline, the title character of Henry Selick's 2009 animated film, has a mom, yet still she imagines having a different one. A better one—one who doesn't have to work, who always pays attention to her and her every desire. The "Other Mother" Coraline meets in a through-the-looking-glass version of her own home offers exactly what Coraline seems to want: a child-fantasy version of reality. A world that's sweeter, more indulgent, and more fun. She presents herself as the perfect alternative to Coraline's real parents, who are distracted and often busy with their own adult lives.

The Other Mother tempts Coraline with a world full of perfect omelets and hot chocolate, watercolor painting and needlepoint, a house that is clean and interesting, and best of all, a place where

Coraline is the absolute center of attention. Sounds like the best childhood ever, right? But there's a price for being the center of the Other Mother's world. (There's always a price.) All Coraline has to do is sew buttons over her eyes, like those on the Other Mother. In the end, Coraline realizes that giving up her own vision of her own life is too steep a cost—for mother and for daughter.

As parents, we worry that we're not good enough. We feel our fallibility every day: we overreact, we lose our temper, we get preoccupied or overwhelmed, we forget things. Sometimes, like Coraline's parents, we miss something that's important to our children and we let them down. At those moments, pause and remember this: the parents who obsessively build their child a world of never-ending, picture-perfect Norman Rockwell moments are constructing a fantasy and, in the process, becoming blind to what their child's reality looks like. After all, it's Coraline's real parents, distracted as they may be by jobs and bills and problems, who have raised a daughter brave and resourceful enough to face the Other Mother and rescue her family.

IT DOESN'T TAKE A BLOOD CONNECTION TO LOVE A CHILD AS YOUR OWN PRINCESS.

D isney's live-action film *Maleficent* is a wicked twist on the familiar fairy tale of Sleeping Beauty: Boy loves fairy girl. Fairy girl loves boy. Boy betrays girl, cuts off her wings, and becomes king. Girl curses boy's baby daughter to die by spindle, but eventually comes to love her like her own child. Girl and daughter save each other. Boy falls to a rocky death. Love wins. New family created.

We often head into adulthood with steadfast opinions about what kind of family we want to be a part of: a partner and two kids, no partner and one kid, a partner and a dog, neither partner nor children but total control over a kingdom as evil dictator, or some other configuration. But life doesn't always work out the way we plan. Sometimes "true love" surprises us.

Maleficent watches over Aurora's childhood to make sure the girl's incompetent fairy godmothers don't inadvertently allow her to get hurt before Maleficent's curse on the girl can go into effect. She's determined to punish Aurora's father, King Stefan, for his brutal betrayal, and hurting his daughter promises to be the perfect revenge. But as Maleficent interacts with the child and watches her grow up, the heart-hardened fairy's malevolent watchfulness evolves into genuine affection.

Maleficent's journey isn't a typical path to motherhood, but it does illustrate the point that there are many different kinds of families and different ways that kids come into our lives. Our partner may have children from a previous relationship. We may become guardians after the death of a loved one. Perhaps we found ourselves ready to have a child without a partner in our lives, or we decided to add to our family by fostering or adopting. Each scenario presents challenges as we attempt to reshape our world to make room for the physical and emotional needs of a new young member. It's not easy, but then neither is parenthood.

Whatever our particular family looks like, it's good for kids to know that there are countless other examples. By talking with them about the ways people shape and reshape their families, we can open their minds to possibilities that may include blended families, multigenerational homes, or polyamorous relationships. Regardless of the characteristics, a family possesses something even more powerful than fairy-tale magic: a home where they are protected and nurtured. However our children come into our lives, Maleficent reminds us that loving a child is an immeasurable and transformative blessing well worth the sacrifice.

THE MORAL OF TODAY'S STORY IS: MAKE TIME TO LAUGH.

Babies can spontaneously smile from birth, and most children begin to laugh by three months old. The first few times they do it, it surprises them because they're not quite sure what's happening with their bodies. But they quickly adapt and delight in the phenomenon. As do we. The squeals of infants and giggles of toddlers are infectious.

Laughter is such a commonality across the human life span that it's surprising we don't have more cartoons like *Animaniacs*, intended to be funny for children and adults alike. A combination of clever jokes, cheeky puns, situational gags, and playful songs, *Animaniacs* engages the audience's sense of humor on many levels. Kids enjoy the slapstick and silliness; grown-ups appreciate the parody and pop culture references. The animated sketch comedy show was the collaboration of Steven Spielberg and Warner Brothers Animation, and it featured the fictional Warner brothers, Yakko and Wakko, and their sister Dot, under the supervision of studio psychiatrist Dr. Otto Scratchansniff. As his efforts to subdue the Warner siblings' zaniness are repeatedly thwarted, Dr. Scratchansniff develops a genuine affection for the kids and even joins in their antics. The Warners teach the good doctor—and us— that laughter triumphs over decorum.

The truth is that most children could teach their parents a few things about laughter. The average child laughs approximately three hundred times a day, whereas the average adult laughs fewer than twenty times in the same time frame. As we get older, we seem to lose our sense of humor—yet the older we get, the more we need laughter. Studies continue to reveal the systemic benefits to the body: how laughter decreases blood pressure, strengthens the immune system, reduces stress hormones, increases alertness and memory. It has even been shown to positively affect healing.

Laughter is something we all need, but it rarely happens when we are alone. An inherently social phenomenon, laughter requires the presence of other people, even if it's only the perception of their presence (on the phone, a computer screen, TV set, etc.). Fortunately, our kids are expert laughers, and they are usually eager for us to laugh along with them. They're our own personal Animaniacs, after all.

Calvin and his parents teach us:

JUST BECAUSE THEY BUILD SNOWMAN MURDER-INVESTIGATION SCENES DOESN'T MEAN THERE'S SOMETHING WRONG WITH THEM.

reshly fallen snow has pristine, untouched potential, like a blank canvas. Our kids look at all that white and cannot wait to charge outside to manifest some imagined landscape: a magic castle with unicorn sentries, a rebel base on Hoth, or—if our kid is the star of *Calvin and Hobbes*—a frozen apocalypse peopled with snowman horror-movie scenes. Like most children, Bill Watterson's comic-strip protagonist Calvin creates pretend personas to act out his fantasies and work out his frustrations: Stupendous Man! Spaceman Spiff! Tracer Bullet! Calvin's parents generally take his actions in stride and with good humor. But what would happen to Calvin if he were a real boy today, dreaming up Deranged Mutant Killer Monster Snow Goons in an era when school systems are perhaps more gun-shy than ever about odd nonconformists?

Our lives, and teachers' lives, would certainly be easier if kids didn't challenge authority. But do we really want neat rows of children following orders, reciting answers, and never asking any distracting questions? It sounds pretty great, but seems just a few short steps away from *Nineteen Eighty-Four* or *Brave New World*. Maybe young readers are hungry for dystopian tales that depict the horror of extreme conformity because sometimes they feel like we're steering them in that direction.

Our world needs more creative thinkers and visionaries, not fewer. Which is why Calvin's parents are such good role models, offering common sense and calm guidance that reins in Calvin's imagination when necessary, without quashing it. Because it's the children with adventurous spirits who will go off into the unknown, to answer the call of Calvin's last line in the final strip of the series: "Let's go exploring."

THERE'S THE FAMILY YOU'RE BORN WITH, AND THEN THERE'S THE FAMILY YOU CLIMB ONBOARD SHIP WITH.

S o many science-fiction shows place human beings into a galactic melting pot filled with an array of different aliens. But not Joss Whedon's much-beloved TV series *Firefly*. His space Western is set in a 'verse populated only with humans who have settled on nearby terraformed planets. It's not an enlightened future à la Gene Roddenberry. Whedon takes the best and worst of life on Earth and projects it all up into space to explore the human condition—specifically, the ways we tear ourselves apart but also come together.

As the captain of the ship *Serenity*, Malcolm Reynolds is responsible for the welfare of his crew—and Zoë Washburne is his second in command. Zoë and Mal have been friends since their days as "Browncoats" fighting for the Independence in the Unification War against the Alliance. Cool-headed Zoë is a good foil to Mal's emotional impetuousness, and together they form the parental figures of *Serenity*'s dysfunctional family. "One of you is gonna fall and die," Mal warns one day, "and I'm not cleaning it up." He's tough but he's fair, and he would do anything for his crew. Zoë is also fiercely loyal, refusing to leave Mal behind when he chooses to go down with the ship. She marries *Serenity*'s kind and geeky pilot Hoban "Wash" Washburne, and though Wash grows jealous of the close friendship shared by Zoë and Mal, theirs is a strong and passionate marriage on a show that revolves around relationships.

Whether celebrating Simon's birthday with a lopsided chocolate protein-paste-frosted cake or enjoying Kaylee's fresh-baked rolls, we see the crew sharing meal after meal gathered around *Serenity*'s communal dining table: bickering, teasing, laughing, and comforting one another.

It's the luck of the draw that determines whom we share blood with. Sometimes we're fortunate, and our birth families are loving and like-minded. Other times we realize as adults that even if we keep ties to the kin of our birth, we'll have to seek out the people who will become our chosen family. The circles of friends that parents gather around themselves are children's first blueprint of how they can someday build their own tribes of kindred spirits. It's not a bad lesson to teach our kids that all sorts of people can become important parts of our lives.

Life is hard on *Serenity*, and survival depends on collaboration. As one former compatriot tells Zoë: "When you can't run, you crawl. And when you can't crawl—" At which Zoë chimes in: "You find someone to carry you."

FIND AN ALTERNATE UNIVERSE WHERE YOU DON'T REPEAT YOUR PARENTS' MISTAKES.

When Dr. Walter Bishop of *Fringe* rips a hole in the multiverse, he is grieving for his son Peter, who died of an illness that even Walter's genius and resources were unable to cure. In his sorrow, Walter finds a universe where his counterpart is about to face the same heartache. Walter travels to the other universe, kidnaps its version of Peter, and brings him back to cure him. Having Peter with him again, even an alternate-reality version, proves too great a temptation, and Walter decides to keep the boy, raising him as his own. Like Dr. Frankenstein, Walter sees himself above the laws of humans and science, performing unorthodox and ethically questionable experiments for the sake of the results. Peter, for his part, shares his father's curiosity and intensity, but ultimately chooses to act differently when it comes to his own child.

The closest thing most of us have to a parenting instruction manual are the examples of our parents. We tend to internalize what we see them do—but that doesn't mean we're doomed to repeat it. We can reflect upon our experiences and recognize the missteps, rejecting those lessons that were not helpful. Like Peter, we can look critically at the way we were raised and choose to redefine our expectations and our actions.

As the Fringe Division, Walter, Peter, Olivia, and Astrid work together on bizarre cases that cannot be solved using regular channels of law enforcement. *Fringe* quickly grows beyond its *X-Files*-esque monster-of-the week storyline, and at the core of the TV show's 100 episodes lies the theme of family: the relationships of Peter and Walter, Peter and Olivia, Olivia and Walter, and their doubles in the alternate universe—"Fauxlivia" and "Walternate"—and the eventual meeting of Olivia and Peter's grown-up daughter Etta in season five.

By the end of the series, Peter and Walter have spent time agonizing over the actions that brought them together and propelled them to the critical juncture that faces their worlds. When Peter chooses a different path from his father, it reminds us that experience is not fate. We can make a conscious effort to break patterns of destructive behavior. And if our children decide to someday become parents, hopefully we will have given them healthier and happier models to draw upon.

2

~~~~~~~~~~~~~~~~

A WORLD OF
TIGERS AND DRAGONS*

Training and equipping them for a life of adventure.

* "Giang Hu is a world of tigers and dragons, full of corruption."
—Li Mu Bai, *Crouching Tiger, Hidden Dragon*

EVEN KINDERGARTENERS HAVE THE POWER TO HELP SAVE THE DAY.

We all start out with preconceptions about the kinds of parents we'll be and the kinds of kids we'll raise. In the *Powerpuff Girls* cartoons, Professor Utonium has his ideas of what makes the "perfect little girl"—sugar, spice, the traditional spiel. But the accidental introduction of a mysterious Chemical X muddies his recipe, and in short order the professor finds himself parent to three strong-minded superpowered kindergarteners.

The brilliant but clumsy prof gladly takes on the paternal tasks of making their lunches and tucking them in. But he also accepts the more nuanced responsibility of mentoring and supporting Blossom, Bubbles, and Buttercup as their heroic abilities are called upon to save the people of Townsville. It's a call the three girls are always happy to answer because of a simple truth: *Little kids want to be big.* Almost from their first steps, kids look around and see a world of people older and stronger who are having adventures, making rules, deciding what's important. Much of the anger and aggression we see when children act out is a frustrated response to feeling helpless and powerless.

Like Professor Utonium, it's part of our job to introduce our kids to the powers they're growing into. We can help them assert control over their world by giving them age-appropriate challenges and choices, like assisting as we make pancakes or asking them to fold laundry. Sure, the pancakes may contain bits of eggshell and the laundry will likely be wrinkled, but exhibiting immediate mastery is not the point. What's important is for children to internalize the effort, to learn how practice will lead them toward triumph.

THEY NEED DISCIPLINE TO DO THEIR HOMEWORK—EVEN IF THAT MEANS EXILING THEM TO A FORTRESS OF SOLITUDE.

R un faster than a speeding bullet? Check. Bend steel with bare hands? Yup. Leap tall buildings in a single bound? No problem. All that stuff is under control. But stop General Zod, another surviving Kryptonian with godlike super-strength, from leading a violent super-army to terrorize the whole of planet Earth? Turns out, that one's not so easy, even for Superman. It's then the question becomes: Hey, Clark, have you done your homework?

It's a truth we're shown time after time: even Superman's amazing inborn powers aren't always enough to enable him to save the day just by flexing and winging it. Sometimes the forces standing against him make for such a colossal challenge, the Man of Steel needs to step back from the frantic urgency of the emergency, collect his thoughts, and marshal his resources. That's when he retreats to his Fortress of Solitude. The Arctic sanctuary built of alien crystal holds all the

surviving knowledge of Superman's home planet, Krypton, archived in databanks carefully preserved by his father, Jor-El. It's an invaluable reference library that Kal-El can turn to in times of need.

For all his herculean muscle and lightning-fast mind, Superman is still much like every middle schooler you've ever known, occasionally in need of a blunt reminder to practice his problem-solving skills *before* the pop quiz suddenly lands on his desk. Like Jor-El, you can't do the work for your kids, but you can prepare a good environment for them to work in. You can build a sanctuary out of daily routine: early on, set a regular evening time frame that children will come to think of as normal studying time. Acclimate them when they're young to the idea that a quiet, library-like space is a happy place.

To help reinforce this space and time as a positive experience, when possible grab your book or laptop and work quietly beside them—just having the company of a parent can encourage concentration and dedication to a task well done. Even Jor-El occasionally pops in to check on his son, albeit holographically. Plus, if you start to see their eyes glazing over with sleepiness or boredom, you'll be on hand to suggest a little study break.

Sophie Hatter and Markl teach us:

WHETHER WIZARD OR HATTER, MANNERS MATTER.

I n Hayao Miyakazi's animated feature *Howl's Moving Castle*—and the Diana Wynne Jones novel upon which the film is based—Sophie Hatter is cursed by the Witch of the Waste to look like a crone. Horrified, Sophie seeks out the infamous wizard Howl for help. She befriends Markl, Howl's apprentice, and Calcifer, the fire-demon who lives in the hearth that fuels Howl's domicile. Appalled at the state of the filthy magical moving castle they call home, and at the atrocious manners of its inhabitants, Sophie gets to work trying to straighten them both out. She begins by sweeping and washing and soon transforms the space into an inviting sanctuary. Then she turns her attention to the manners of young Markl, who uses dirty silverware, shovels his food into his mouth, and chews with his mouth open.

Reluctant at first, Howl and Markl begin to respond to Sophie's efforts. Howl adds new rooms to the castle to make Sophie more comfortable, and

Markl treats her with greater respect. Before too long their improved, tidy, and harmonious surroundings reflect the group's shift from chaotic castlemates into a caring family. They even welcome their enemy, the Witch of the Waste, into their home. Good manners help reshape both their space and their behavior.

We teach our kids from an early age that there is a proper way to act at the table, or in a guest's home, or when meeting other people. But it's important to instruct them not only *how* they should behave, but also *why*. Rules of etiquette aren't just antiquated systems of formal behavior; manners are a show of respect for other people. Gestures such as making eye contact, shaking hands, picking up after ourselves, treating objects with care, and waiting for everyone to receive their meal before we eat are all visible acts that show other people that we recognize and appreciate them.

As our children grow and go out into the world, manners can help them tread carefully and speak thoughtfully when they encounter a diversity of people, customs, and expectations. By teaching our children to be polite, what we're really doing is encouraging them to treat all people—those within their own communities as well as outside of them—with the respect and courtesy that we all deserve.

Meg Murray and Aunt Beast teach us:

DON'T JUDGE FOOD—OR ANYTHING ELSE—BY ITS APPEARANCE.

All too often, children get into a rut of wanting to eat only their few favorite dishes. Anything that looks, smells, or tastes out of the ordinary is summarily rejected. In a world full of such delicious things, how do we help finicky little eaters cultivate an appreciation of different kinds of foods?

In Madeleine L'Engle's classic 1963 novel *A Wrinkle in Time*, the children learn they cannot judge anything by appearance alone. The "turkey" feast served to Meg Murry, her brother Charles Wallace, and their friend Calvin on the planet Camazotz seems to look and taste delicious. But that's only because IT, the giant brain that rules the alien world, is mentally controlling the flavor sensors in the brains of every person on the planet. Unhypnotized, Charles Wallace finds that the pretty but synthetic food in fact tastes like sand. In contrast, after teleporting via tesseract to the nearby planet of Ixchel, Meg meets Aunt Beast. The food presented is "dull and colorless and unappetizing to look at," but it turns out to be some of the most delicious they have ever tasted.

Our children watch us to see what we eat. As with many things, we must educate by example: we can't expect them to be adventurous eaters if they don't see us trying an array of foods. If we expose them to as much variety as possible, we help them see that the world is full of more than macaroni, chicken nuggets, and carrot sticks. It would be unrealistic to expect kids to eat and enjoy all the different foods we offer. But if we encourage our young gourmands to at least sample some new edibles now and then, they'll broaden their palate at their own pace. And they'll learn that amazing discoveries can be made if, like Aunt Beast, they don't get distracted by what things look like.

The Parr family teaches us:

CLOTHES DON'T MAKE THE HERO, CHARACTER DOES. BUT STILL, DRESS FOR SUCCESS.

Bob Parr, a.k.a. Mr. Incredible, didn't feel like himself anymore. He squeezed into a boring button-down shirt every day and tried to be a dutiful office worker, but Bob knew his proper vocation: *superhero.* So when a secret agent calls him back into action, one of his first steps is to knock on the door of Edna Mode, superhero fashion-designer extraordinaire. Freshly dressed as the Incredible he always knew himself to be, Bob leaps back into the fray. Before long, his entire family is outfitted to match and throwing punches by his side.

Most of us don't have an Edna Mode on retainer, someone whose fashion helps transform us into heroes. But every outfit is a costume we put on to assume a special identity that comes with its own powers. We use clothing to convince the world—and ourselves—that we're adults.

Kids need to learn the secret powers of these everyday "costumes." Dress for an incredible future and feel your body standing taller. Choosing clothes that help turn you into who you want to be is a superpower in itself.

Jen, Jade Fox, and Shu Lien teach us:

A GIRL WITH A SWORD ISN'T A "TOMBOY." SHE'S A GIRL. WITH A SWORD.

T he women of *Crouching Tiger, Hidden Dragon,* one of the first *Wuxia* films to achieve widespread acclaim in the West, push the boundaries of what's traditionally considered acceptible for women in Western action films. Jen Yu, the daughter of a visiting Manchu aristocrat, is envious of warrior woman Shu Lien's lifestyle. Jen has been secretly studying martial arts with the infamous Jade Fox, who is posing as her governess. Jen begins the film embracing the camaraderie of both women. But by the story's end, Jen's desire for power makes her push away Shu Lien, and Jen's superior skill alienates her from Jade Fox. After Shu Lien's beloved Li Mu Bai dies— as a result of Jen's actions—she says to Jen: "Promise me one thing. Whatever path you take . . . be true to yourself."

These three women defy stereotypes. Expectations about gender are all around us, and we often fall in step with them as soon as our children's biological sex is known. But in reality, not all people fall into those prescribed roles. Like Jen, our children will want to explore who they are. If we stand in their way because they confound our expectations, they'll find a way to do it on the sly. Better to let them know that what we most want is what Shu Lien wishes for Jen: for them be true to themselves.

Data and Jean-Luc Picard ask us:

INQUIRY: ARE YOU ENCOURAGING THEM TO ASK QUESTIONS?

In *Star Trek: The Next Generation,* Lieutenant Commander Data is an android created by one of Starfleet's leading cyberneticists, Dr. Noonian Soong. Data has the chance to meet his creator only a few times. A more formative influence in his development is Data's ongoing friendship with Captain Jean-Luc Picard. A wise and empathetic mentor, Picard takes the time to respond to Data's frequent questioning, even arguing with his Starfleet superiors for Data's rights as a sentient being. Whereas Dr. Soong had a predetermined plan for Data to become as much like a human as possible, Picard encourages Data to figure things out for himself. And so, like a child, Data tries to make sense of the world around him and his place in it through careful observation and thoughtful questions.

When they are young, children ask us questions because they're trying to identify and name things, categorize them, make connections. They are like little scientists (or newly constructed self-aware androids) trying to understand the

rules. That phase of a hundred daily "whys" (Why is the sky blue? Why are there rainbows after a storm? Why do I have to go to sleep?) is short-lived, but it's not the only time when inquisitiveness matters. Children experience different stages of learning as they develop, and questions play a key role in each. Questioning is a sign of intelligence, whether you're a preschooler, a middle grader, a college student, or an android with a positronic brain. The quickest way to shut down a child's curiosity is to make them feel foolish for asking something. There are no dumb questions.

As kids grow older, they pose us fewer questions. It's hard for tweens and preteens to admit they don't know something. When they do come to us with an inquiry, they make themselves vulnerable and show they value our opinions. At those moments, we may pine for the "Why is the sky blue?" days. But hang in there. Once children become teenagers and young adults, the role of questions shifts again. Now each query becomes an invitation, an opportunity to exchange ideas, knowledge, and perception. Not having an answer at the ready is nothing to be embarrassed about. Just like Captain Picard patiently fielding Data's queries, searching for the answers is an opportunity to explore strange new worlds together.

Dana, Kevin, and Rufus teach us:

THE WORLD IS NOT FAIR, BUT ALL HUMANS ARE KINDRED.

n Octavia Butler's classic 1979 time-travel novel *Kindred*, Dana Franklin finds herself sent back in time, a black woman from 1970s America transported to a plantation in the antebellum South. She's "called" to the past several times to save the life of one of her ancestors, Rufus Weylin, a white slaveowner. She travels back and forth in history, and on a subsequent trip is accompanied by her white husband, Kevin. Given the time and place, the interracial couple is forced into a dangerous pantomime, with Dana posing as Kevin's property. Kevin's social status as a white man allows him to imagine all sorts of "really fascinating" historical time periods. But for Dana, there aren't many American eras in which being both black and a woman wouldn't put her life and freedom at far greater risk than his.

That's a sort of privilege the well-meaning Kevins of the world often have not considered: No matter how hard their lives have been, the exact same life would have been *even harder* if lived with the extra pressures that society adds with every notch a person varies from the "norm" of being "white, thin, male, young, heterosexual, Christian, financially secure."

Kids develop an early understanding that the world ought to be "fair." Adults know that the world is *not* fair. Justice is a goal we strive for, not a state we live in. Going back in time may not be an option (yet). But the more we show our kids the unfair consequences of valuing whiteness over color, men over women, wealth over poverty, and so on, the better chance they will relate to the common humanity of us all. And the more likely they will grow up to be adults who recognize the shared responsibility in working to make the world more just.

TAKE-YOUR-CHILD-TO-WORK DAY IS ONE OF THE MORE IMPORTANT TRADITIONS FOR A SUPER-PARENT TO HONOR.

L ike Buffy Summers of *Buffy the Vampire Slayer* and Claire Bennet of *Heroes*, Kim Possible is a cheerleader-turned-heroine. She's a renaissance teenager: a good athlete and honor student whose freelance around-the-world heroism is well known and respected among her peers. Her mother, Ann Possible (a.k.a. Mrs. Dr. P.), is also a hero in her own right. Even as one of the world's foremost brain surgeons, Mrs. Dr. P. still makes time for her daughter. She might be wrist-deep inside someone's skull when her daughter calls to ask for advice, but she takes that call, even if she has to put Kim on speakerphone.

In the episode "Mother's Day," Kim and Mrs. Dr. P. plan to spend the entire day together, but Mrs. Dr. P. is called in to perform an emergency surgery. Kim, though momentarily disappointed, is soon awed by the intensity of the operating room. "I had no idea how major your job is," she tells her mom. "I mean it's, it's . . . well, it's brain surgery."

Getting a glimpse into her mother's adult life gives Kim a whole new perspective on what is possible for a person to accomplish. Sure, kids know that their parents work, and they probably know the one-line description of what their job is. But how many know exactly what it is their parents *actually do* all day long? How many have an understanding of just how complicated a web of daily achievements is involved in producing the paychecks that keep the family going?

We do our kids a disservice if we let them think grown-up life is easy—ours, or anyone's, regardless of who they are. Though we want them to feel safe and secure, we don't want them to develop a skewed sense of what it means to be a responsible, functioning adult.

It's worth noting that Kim's motto is "I can do anything," not "I can do everything." There is a difference, and it's an important one to learn. We want to encourage our children to dream big and work hard—but we should also let them see some of the compromises and sacrifices that go into making dreams come true. If they see what our daily quest for success looks like, our kids are much more likely to keep trying to succeed. And should they happen to see us bouncing back from a setback, well, that's a more valuable lesson than thinking their parents never encounter any challenges.

DON'T LET YOUR ROYAL HEIR TRY TO PUSH AROUND THE SEVEN KINGDOMS.

A dolescents and teens inevitably see the ways that power is distributed. They start to question: Who has the power at home, at school, in the world? Who is powerless? Why? How can *they* get power, and what would they do with it? At this stage, our children test boundaries to see where they can gain control. Sometimes that manifests itself as exerting power over those who are less powerful than they are.

In the 2010s *Game of Thrones* saga, Joffrey Baratheon is a classic bully who boasts the added muscle of sitting on the iron throne. A sadistic boy given too much authority and not enough guidance, Joffrey lacks empathy and is quick to blame and shame others. His egomania comes as no surprise: Joffrey's mother, Cersei Lannister, trapped in a loveless and abusive marriage, devotes her life to her children. She shares the opinion of her husband, King Robert Baratheon, that royalty can do whatever it likes.

Joffrey wants what he wants, and woe to those who try to deny him; it's the attitude of a toddler. As parents, we must guide our kids out of this mindset, giving them the tools to become humane adults. By focusing on humanity and compassion, we show that one doesn't have to be a bully to get things done. Instead, children can cultivate healthy and happy relationships to build what they need.

Lee Wagstaff and Bayou teach us:

KNOWLEDGE IS POWER; WE SHOULD RAISE POWERFUL CHILDREN.

I n the graphic novel *Bayou,* Lee Wagstaff is the latest in a long line of fictional girls who enter fantasy worlds looking for adventure. Lee goes in search of a rabbit, but the stakes in her quest are much more poignant than those faced by Lewis Carroll's Alice in her wonderland.

When Lee's white friend, Lily Westmoreland, is kidnapped by an evil supernatural entity, it's Lee's father, a black share-cropper, who is unjustly accused and imprisoned. Armed with a blessed Choctaw axe given by her uncle, Lee enters the mythic swamplands wilderness to find her missing playmate. While there, she befriends a compassionate creature named Bayou.

Lee's father doesn't hide the truth of the racism and injustice that shape their lives. Keeping kids in the dark about the world's horrors, though understandable, may hinder them later. Better to arm them—at the appropriate age—with information that allows for the development of confident and strong convictions, just like those of brave Lee.

Bayou is the kind of book, and parental lesson, that's painful to experience. It presents an allegory for deeply rooted racism that still colors and destroys many children's lives. We never want to scare our kids, but sometimes the world is a scary place. It's up to them to continue working toward solutions.

Tyler and Rendell Locke teach us:

BEFORE YOU HAND THEM THE KEYS, MAKE SURE THEY KNOW HOW TO USE THEM.

F or a child, keys are like magic. As soon as they're handed one, they begin to wonder where it came from, what it unlocks. Keys open doors, but they also lead to mysteries. They symbolize the potential of things unknown, the possibility of adventure.

In Joe Hill and Gabriel Rodriguez's comic-book series Locke & Key, the Locke kids and their mother move to Keyhouse Manor after the gruesome murder of their father. It is at their father's ancestral home in Lovecraft, Massachusetts, that the family tries to deal with the trauma and loss—especially oldest brother Tyler, who feels responsible for his dad's death. As the children explore the house, they discover keys of unusual shapes and properties, as well as the mysterious doors they unlock. Tyler's younger brother Bode finds the first, the Ghost Key, which allows him to leave his body and wander as a spirit. There are many others—Bitey Key, Echo Key, Anywhere Key, Hercules Key—that, it turns out, have been used by generations of Locke children to access powers and portals. Tyler Locke starts out as an angry, frightened teenager but eventually grows into his role as the mature protector of his family. That growth comes at a great cost.

Many rites of passage are connected to keys. When kids get their first bicycle, they need a key to lock it up. When they're old enough to walk home from school, they get the keys to open the house. Giving them keys is a sign of trust and maturity. From fictional powers of the gods to the very real power of driving a car, keys can unlock amazing possibilities. With a little help from us, the keymasters, kids will understand that when those keys are used irresponsibly, the consequences can be devastating.

San and Moro teach us:

IF YOU WANT THEM TO HELP SAVE THE EARTH, YOU HAVE TO TEACH THEM TO LOVE THE EARTH.

When we first meet San, the warrior princess has blood all over her mouth as she sucks poison from the wound of the majestic white wolf goddess who raised her. This is no dainty Disney princess: San, also known as Princess Mononoke, is fierce and feral. And she will protect her home—the forest—with her life.

Nature gives us moments of transcendent beauty and tranquility: rainbows and waterfalls, sunsets and fields of flowers. Nature is also indiscriminately ferocious and violent, with tsunamis and tornados, thunderstorms and animal attacks. The relationship between humanity and the Earth is a complicated one, and that is the remarkable beauty of Hayao Miyazaki's 1997 animated film *Princess Mononoke*. It demonstrates the many facets of our relationship with the majestic, and sometimes brutal, natural world.

The ancient wolf goddess Moro discovers San's parents damaging the forest and attacks them. In an attempt to save their lives, San's parents throw their baby daughter to Moro as a sacrifice. Rather than kill her, Moro raises San as her own. As a result, San regards Moro as her mother and Moro's two pups as brothers. And like her adopted mother, San's main concern in life is to protect the forest and her family.

San and Moro remind us that we, too, are a part of nature. If we teach our children to regard this planet with the kind of respect and reverence we reserve for family, they will be on the way to helping build a sustainable future. Like the people of Irontown, we need to find a way to survive, which sometimes means drawing on natural resources, but those resources aren't infinite.

In *Princess Mononoke*, the spirits of nature turn against humanity, attempting to restore some kind of balance after people stop heeding their warnings. Alarmingly, we see conflicts play out in the real world that feel all too similar: oil spills, rainforest destruction, species loss, health issues relating to contaminated water and food sources. Our kids are likely to inherit some of our environmental mistakes. But if we teach the lessons of San and Moro, they'll hopefully also inherit a passion for the natural world that will lead them to become caretakers of the planet, not just consumers of its bounty.

Nell and Miranda teach us:

LET THEM READ DANGEROUS BOOKS.

Why do authorities sometimes try to ban books? Because books are dangerous: they show us compelling ways the world could be different than it is. In Neal Stephenson's 1995 science-fiction classic *The Diamond Age*, the evolution of the Net and the disintegration of nation-states result in humanity dividing itself into tribal zones. The story introduces us to a dangerous book titled *The Interactive Young Lady's Illustrated Primer* that's meant to encourage independent and subversive thought.

The cyberbook bonds with its owner, so when a copy falls into the hands of a poor girl named Nell, she becomes the star of her Primer—read to her by Miranda, a remote actor, or "ractor." Miranda becomes a surrogate mother and teacher to Nell: she instructs the girl how to read, write, and think independently. However, the Primer alone isn't enough to transform a girl into a revolutionary. Although Nell picks up on its subversive message, two other girls reading the same book have dramatically different experiences. Words can call a reader to action, but it's up to each individual to respond or not.

Books don't have to be sexual, horrific, religious, or political to be deemed threatening. In truth, any book that challenges an accepted way of thinking can be regarded as a threat by someone. Books that instruct us how to do things, books that teach controversial beliefs, books that tell stories of people who have been silenced or erased . . . these are "dangerous" in all the best ways. Such books are banned by organizations or nations. They are removed from schools or hidden, and sometimes they are burned, their authors threatened with physical harm.

In reality, we can't stop children from reading books we don't approve of. If we're of the opinion that a child is not quite ready for a book, we can try to delay their reading it. But when young people decide they really want to read something, it's highly unlikely we can permanently block their efforts. Remember your own scavenging for provocative books in your youth? And that was before the Internet. Kids will get their hands on the things they want to read, whether or not they, or we, are ready. Attempts at keeping the "wrong" books out of their hands are fruitless. Instead, we should save our energy for thoughtful discussions when they come to us with questions about the new ideas they've discovered.

Samantha Stephens and Endora teach us:

ENCOURAGE YOUR KIDS NOT TO HIDE IN THE BROOM CLOSET. WHATEVER KIND OF WITCHES THEY ARE, THEY CAN OWN THEIR POWER.

The 1960s were a decade of high-concept sitcoms, several of which boasted a supernatural spin. These TV shows gave audiences a fantasy or science-fiction lens through which to view the world, one in the midst of profound social change. Against a backdrop of folklore and time travel, witches and warlocks, *Bewitched* tackled stereotypes, challenged heteronormative social codes, and provided a look at some of the challenges that women of that era were facing.

The hook was simple: What happens when a powerful witch marries an ordinary, suburban ad man? Until then, men had been the heads of household and leaders of industry, and Samantha's husband Darrin buys into many of those patriarchal assumptions. In fact, it's his job to sell that message to the masses. He wants Samantha to forsake her magic talents, but the times are changing; women are fighting against limitations put on their careers and relationships. And so, while watching *Bewitched*, we laugh—and reflect—as Samantha struggles to reconcile her power as a woman and a witch with the expectations of middle-class America.

Like any parent watching their child struggle, Samantha's mother Endora cannot understand why her daughter would give up the infinite majesty of a magical life. Frequently echoing the language of the feminist Betty Friedan, Endora criticizes the tedium of housework and her daughter's suburban prison. She takes every opportunity to remind Samantha of her right to be a force in the world, despite anything "what's-his-name" may say to the contrary.

But now it's the twenty-first century, more than fifty years since *Bewitched* cast its spell. Surely we've gotten past issues like workplace equality and women's rights to control their bodies. Sadly, no, we haven't. The U.S. Constitution still does not guarantee equal rights to women. Also unresolved are the complex and interconnected relationships between gender, race, and class that were largely ignored by the white feminists of the 1960s.

Parents today continue to be met with resistance as we try to raise healthy, strong, intelligent girls. We need to make sure that our daughters hear us over all the other voices that tell them to change how they look, to play dumb, to speak more softly, to be less than they are. We also need to guarantee that our sons don't join that chorus of negativity. Like Endora, we want to raise girls who do not hide. Girls who own their power, whether it's intelligence, athletic prowess, empathy, wit, creativity, or anything else that gives them strength.

Luka, Soraya, and Rashid Khalifa teach us:

PLAYING GAMES CAN BE SERIOUS BUSINESS.

Our children have more computer power at their fingertips as toddlers than we had in junior high. At times, that technology may seem like an abyss between us. How can we relate to kids who spend so much time typing and swiping their way through digital space? It's a different reality than the one we grew up in, but if we want to stay connected, we need to get to know it. We can't just expect our children to appreciate our world without taking the time to understand theirs—be it the games they play, the shows they watch, or the language they speak with their friends.

In Salman Rushdie's 2010 novel *Luka and the Fire of Life*, we see an example of the technology generation gap in the relationship of twelve-year-old Luka and his mother, Soraya. Luka is an avid gamer and member of several online communities, but his mother doesn't see the value in that. She says to her husband, Rashid: "In the real world there are no levels, only difficulties. If he makes a careless mistake in the game, he gets another chance. If he makes a careless mistake in a chemistry test he gets a minus mark. Life is tougher than video games." But Rashid praises his son's gaming aptitude—and as it turns out, Luka's video-gaming does have real consequences in the physical world. After Rashid slips into a strange coma,

Luka goes on a quest through the World of Magic to reclaim the Fire of Life for his father. He must navigate whimsical and mythic landscapes—and he's good at it because of his time spent mastering video games. This time, however, the game has much higher stakes, for now he's "playing" to save his father's life.

What seems like just a diversion can often be important in children's development—not just for the joy it brings them, but for the ways it helps cultivate both their imagination and their motor skills. Certainly, we need to make sure our kids don't spend all their time staring at screens. But whether we like it or not, the world is, and will continue to be, shaped by people whose lives are integrated with technology. In *Luka and the Fire of Life*, it's ultimately the combination of Rashid's wordplay and Luka's gameplay that helps Luka rescue his father. Likewise, we need to be able to meet our children in the middle, sharing our world but also letting them share theirs. Because there, in the middle, is where we'll find home.

Remy and Django teach us:

LET THEM PLAY WITH THEIR FOOD—IN THE KITCHEN.

Remy—the adorable rat in the 2007 film *Ratatouille*—has a refined sense of smell and taste, a sardonic wit, and a passion for cooking. He dreams of becoming a gourmet chef, like the famous Auguste Gusteau. So, unlike his father and brother—who are content to eat scraps straight from the trash—Remy combines the flavors he finds while foraging to make savory culinary discoveries. His father, Django, chastises him for his fanciful ideas: "Food is fuel. You get picky about what you put in the tank, your engine is gonna die. Now shut up and eat your garbage." But for Remy, food is his art.

Children love to play, and the kitchen is an excellent place for creative amusement that teaches them important skills. If we start them early—washing fruit, making toast, pouring their cereal and milk—kids gain confidence in basic culinary tasks. If we allow them to watch and assist us preparing food, we encourage their curiosity. If we give them opportunities to taste and smell fresh herbs and spices, we help develop their palate and enrich our own. Picking a recipe and making it with our kids can be an adventure (albeit a messy one).

Remy is eventually able to introduce his father and brother to the joy of good food and cooking. That's because meals are a delicious kind of magic. Family recipes can connect us with loved ones, both those enjoying the meal with us and those who cooked it in days gone by. The making (or inventing) of a dish can help the entire family work together. And the sharing of a meal can demonstrate the very real ways we are nourished by those we love. Isn't that worth wiping up the counters and washing the dishes?

Buffy Summers and Rupert Giles teach us:

IT TAKES A GILES TO GET THE MOST OUT OF GOOGLE.

Questions abound. Who made the Statue of Liberty? Can a vampire recover his soul? How does one stop a cult worshipping the Old Ones? Our knee-jerk reaction to an important question is probably to google it, but we all know that the results won't necessarily be what we're looking for. Sometimes we need more help than a search engine can offer—especially if, like Buffy Summers, we live in a town built atop a magical evil-luring hellmouth.

A popular cheerleader at Summerdale High, Buffy never expected to be called to serve as the next slayer of paranormal nasties, so not surprisingly she has a lot of questions. Fortunately, Rupert Giles, the school's thoughtful and metaphysically savvy librarian, becomes her Watcher, acting in loco parentis to teach and guide her in her duties. For the first three seasons of the show, Buffy and her friends, the affectionately dubbed "Scooby Gang," meet in the school library to delve into Giles's stacks of books for archaic research about vampires, demons, and other Big Bads.

Many of us can remember when reference materials were limited to a set of encyclopedias at home and a collection of books at the library, but our children are growing up in an age when all the reference materials in the world are accessible in the palm of their hand. But libraries were never just places to go for facts and figures—we also went there to engage in conversations about things we were interested in. Librarians were there to help us. Sometimes they knew the answer off the top of their heads; other times, they guided us to the places where we could find out more. They may point us to the biography of Al Capone in one breath and then suggest a Terry Pratchett novel in the next. No search algorithm can make those kinds of connections.

As the Internet grows, librarians become more important, not less. They still help patrons navigate the physical stacks of books, but these days they also assist us in distinguishing between what's real and true and what's questionable blather. We may not be the parents of little slayers, but hopefully we're raising children who appreciate and value the guardians of knowledge. Librarians show kids new worlds their eyes have never seen—not at random, but with the intent to help them start their science project. Or slay a vampire.

The Little Prince, the Fox, and the Pilot teach us:

YOU BECOME RESPONSIBLE, FOREVER, FOR WHAT YOU HAVE TAMED.

When a pilot crashes in the Sahara Desert, he meets a space alien, a young royal who has been exploring the universe. As the pilot attempts to repair his plane and survive on the dwindling water supply, the little prince entertains him with a retelling of his journey to Earth. The two discover they are kindred spirits—the pilot is delighted that the little prince is able to recognize his drawings, and the little prince is happy to finally meet an adult not as foolish as the inhabitants of other asteroids he's visited. With the passing of days and sharing of stories, their friendship grows. Among his adventures, the little prince recounts meeting a fox who taught him the art of "taming." The fox says: "If you tame me, then we shall need each other. To me, you will be unique in all the world. To you, I shall be unique in all the world."

Published in 1943, Antoine de Saint-Exupéry's charmingly illustrated fable *The Little Prince* is a meditation on friendship, and taming is at the heart of it. Even as he is taming the fox, the little prince realizes that he has been tamed by a very special rose back home, and this makes her more precious than all the roses on planet Earth. It has taken him a year of exploring to realize just how much she means to him. The pilot meets the little prince at the very end of his journey, and even as the little prince is taming the pilot, he is preparing to get bitten by the snake to return home to his beloved on asteroid B612. The little prince has learned that the sorrow of separation is the very thing that teaches us just how precious our time is together.

Our world is filled with inanimate and disposable objects that exist for the sole purpose of entertaining children. But along with plastic animals and dolls and electronic gadgets, kids need things they can nurture, whether it's a goldfish or a garden, backyard chickens or a bonsai tree. The little prince teaches us that the most meaningful things in life are those we take time to care for.

Caring for a living thing teaches kids to consider the needs of something other than themselves. As they become acquainted with a pet, they learn how to feed another creature, handle it gently, and care for it when it gets sick. As they nurture a garden, they experience how fragile the environment is and how interconnected humans are with nature. Whatever they're taming, our children will discover that responsibility and nurturing are crucial to creating a true and lasting connection with the world and its inhabitants.

Prince Akeem, Queen Aeoleon, and King Jaffe Joffer teach us:

RAISE BOYS WHO RESPECT WOMEN—NOT JUST AS QUEENS, BUT AS PEOPLE.

How did Eddie Murphy's 1988 comedy *Coming to America* secure itself a place in a celebration of geek culture? Simple: its romantic leads are both *super* nerdy at heart. Sure, Prince Akeem Joffer, heir to the throne of the African nation of Zamunda, may be a rich, handsome charmer with mad martial arts skills. But he's also a restless intellectual who quotes Nietzsche, trains ninja-style with a *bō* staff, and craves an independent-minded romantic partner to be his friend as well as his queen. The friend in question, Lisa McDowell, applies her math wizardry to run her father's accounting ledgers, geeks out over community charity initiatives, and stands up for her feminist dedication to a free-thinking, nonoppressed life. These two are a nerd wish-fulfillment power couple if ever Hollywood gave us one.

Akeem's matter-of-fact resolve to marry a strong, brainy woman rather than a physically flawless doormat sets him apart from almost every other man in the story. Considering how much casual sexism is displayed by almost all those around him, we are left to conclude that Akeem's mother, the queen, deserves props for having shown her growing son what a no-nonsense woman of power looks like.

The lesson Akeem internalized so successfully in the face of a chauvinist culture is one that every parent would do well to remember. When children understand that women possess equal agency, they are less likely to objectify them, sexually or otherwise. And more likely to interact with all women as fellow humans worthy of respect. So don't let your child think of girls as prizes to be won; show by example that they're thinkers and doers who will think and do whatever they damn well please.

KEEP A DIARY OR TREASURE BOX OF THE HIDDEN GEMS YOU WANT THEM TO EXPLORE SOMEDAY.

We begin with the best of intentions when our children are born, amassing albums for photographs, journals to mark milestones, and memory boxes to be filled with firsts: shoes, teeth, clips of hair, drawings, well-loved baby blankets, and other mementos. We may even remember to put things in those albums and boxes in the beginning. But the older they become, the more likely we will get caught up in the living of life and forget about the recording of it.

Some people are naturals at documentation and journaling. Take Indiana Jones's dad, Henry Jones Sr., a professor of medieval literature who relates better to books than to his son. In 1898, Henry has a vision about the Holy Grail that he records in his diary; from that point on, he travels the world in search of the sacred vessel, taking the diary everywhere and filling its nearly three hundred pages with notes, sculpture rubbings, sketches, train ticket stubs, and maps. Resentful of the time his father devotes to his quest, Indy leaves home to pursue his own archaeological dreams. Father and son remain estranged for many years until Indiana receives his father's diary in the mail. Knowing that Henry would never allow the diary out of his sight unless something was wrong, Indy takes off in search of his dad.

Keepsakes trigger memories: places we've been, things we've experienced, moments we've lived and want to remember. Henry's diary is more than just a collection of clues; it's also a reflection of his life and passion for several decades. Among the precious things Henry saves is an 1899 silver dollar certificate that commemorates the year Indiana was born. Henry does value his son—he just doesn't know how to show him. In the end, the journal is what brings father and son together and helps them find the Holy Grail that saves Henry's life.

It doesn't matter if our mementos are pasted onto pretty handmade paper or collected inside shoeboxes, if they're documented in calligraphy on parchment or scribbled in spiral-bound notebooks. Maybe we're the kind of crafty parent who delights in scrapbooking. If not, that's okay. The important thing is that we remember to save a few gems when we can. Because memories are fleeting and it's easy to forget important moments when time has passed. The real treasure is in the content, not the presentation, and its value only increases when it's shared.

Barbara Gordon and Commissioner James Gordon teach us:

DIFFERENCES MAKE FOR A BETTER TEAM OF SUPERHEROES.

hildren recognize differences: a woman being led by a seeing-eye dog, a girl with a prosthetic arm, a man who walks with an artificial leg. Curious and lacking any filters, kids may stare or ask questions. They aren't being cruel—they're trying to make sense of the world and its rules. So when something looks new or unusual, they take notice. It's up to us as parents to create a context for those differences. How we respond helps shape their attitudes and behavior toward people with disabilities.

For most of the past twenty-five years, the DC Comics character Barbara Gordon, originally (and now once again) known as Batgirl, fought crime under the name Oracle, using her remarkable intellect and abilities. Smart and strong, Oracle is also a superhero in a wheelchair. She challenges us to expand our mental model of what a superhero looks like. Her relationships with other superheroes—as well as with her father, the Gotham police commissioner James Gordon—are based on mutual respect and not defined or hindered by her disability.

Books and movies help expand children's worldviews as well as their imaginations. Sure, certain superheroes have mutated genes, chemically altered physiologies, high-tech power suits, and alien or divine parentage. Some superheroes are confined to wheelchairs, deal with mental illnesses, or are blind. Again and again, we see that the strongest teams are those made up of heroes with the most diverse skills and powers. Yet comic-book worlds reflect only a fraction of the real world's diversity. Oracle reminds us to teach our kids that, just as comics are filled with misfits and mutants who are also heroes, in real life being different does not mean someone can't be extraordinary.

Charlie Bucket and Grandpa Joe teach us:

WE SHOULD SAVOR LIFE'S SWEETNESS, WITH OR WITHOUT A GOLDEN TICKET.

In Roald Dahl's 1964 children's classic *Charlie and the Chocolate Factory*, and the movie versions it inspired, Charlie Bucket lives with his poverty-stricken family in a tiny one-room house, with his Grandpa Joe as his dearest confidante. When Willy Wonka's golden ticket contest is announced, it's Grandpa Joe who seems most excited. After Charlie's first candy bar yields no ticket, Grandpa Joe gives the boy a sixpence from his secret hoard to afford another chance. And when the second Wonka bar also produces no ticket, Charlie and his grandfather still don't despair.

Charlie eventually stumbles across a golden ticket on his own, and it's Grandpa Joe who accompanies him to the factory. Once there, the mad chocolatier puts Charlie and the other winners through an increasingly bizarre series of sugar-fueled, carnival-horror stress tests. But Grandpa Joe and Charlie know how to appreciate all the awe-inspiring moments with wonder instead of greed. Charlie stands out from the rest of the contest-winning cohort. And that's why he's chosen to continue Willy Wonka's chocolate legacy.

THINK CAREFULLY ABOUT THE PRECIOUS THINGS YOUR KIDS WILL INHERIT.

Most of us are mortal. That means the time will come when we leave this life for the mystery of death. Hopefully that will happen when we are old and content. But whatever the timing, we should ask ourselves: What legacy will be left behind?

In J. R. R. Tolkein's classic *The Hobbit*, first published in 1937, Bilbo Baggins is forever changed by his travels with the dwarves and by the ring he took from Gollum. Later he shares those experiences with his nephew. Bilbo bequeaths both his home, Bag End, and his mysterious ring to Frodo. In doing so, Bilbo sets Frodo on an adventure that echoes Bilbo's own before surpassing it in danger and sacrifice.

We may think that by leaving our children worldly goods we are giving them treasures. But we may be burdening them instead. Don't bequeath your child a cursed ring—that much is a no-brainer. But be equally thoughtful of everything else you leave behind. It's not a fun topic, but even Gandalf the Grey didn't know he was going to tumble into that chasm. If he'd left some instructions, the Fellowship of the Ring might have stayed together.

DON'T TRY TO FORCE YOUR KIDS TO FOLLOW IN YOUR FOOTSTEPS.

J oin me, and together we can rule the galaxy as father and son." That's some offer, isn't it? It's easy to see how Darth Vader thought it would be irresistible to young Luke Skywalker. Yet history is littered with talented children of powerful parentage who chose a different path.

Like Darth Vader, every parent feels the lure of crafting a mini-me. But the temptation to see our children as validation for our own existence—that's the real dark side of the Force. It's a parent's job to give our kids the tools for success. Though a well-rounded education may not be a hand-me-down lightsaber, it's pretty much the real-world equivalent of Jedi training for the healthy development of any Padawan. Just be sure not to offer only *one* model, a *single* path. Darth Vader assured the emperor that Luke would "join us or die." Ultimately, he learned the hard way that the opposite was true: his son would rather die than be shoved into a mold that wasn't true to who he was.

Vader learned too late that it's a parent's responsibility to show kids the many possibilities in the universe, to give them the time and space to make their own choices. Sometimes, it's when making a mistake that kids discover who they really are. As Luke did for Vader, they might even show us something valuable about ourselves, too.

Mickey Smith and his Gran teach us:

YOU DON'T NEED A TIME MACHINE TO CREATE A BETTER FUTURE.

octor Who's Mickey Smith starts out as the slapstick, slightly pathetic comic relief to his hero-in-training girlfriend, Rose Tyler. We laugh at his antics, but eventually Mickey realizes that he has a life-crippling problem: he doesn't believe in himself. That epiphany comes when he meets the Doctor's four-legged robot sidekick, K-9, who also lacks ambition. "I'm the tin dog," Mickey laments.

Dissatisfied, Mickey steps forward to join Rose and the Doctor in their time-and-space adventures. When they fall into an alternate universe, Mickey resolves to make hard choices. He decides to remain to care for his mirror-world grandmother, who'd died back home never having seen him act like an adult.

Traveling in the TARDIS may have given Mickey the opportunity to reenvision his life, but battling Cybermen across the timelines isn't what made him a man. It was the realization that he had it within his power to take the reins of his own destiny. So when helping your children struggle with a leveling-up crux point—whether an obvious one ("How should I pursue higher education?") or an open-ended one ("What do I do when bullies are tormenting my friend?")—it may help to remind them that what they decide is important, but accepting the responsibility to make a decision is even more so.

3

~~~~~~~~~~~~~~~~

YOU KNOW
I DON'T LIKE IT WHEN
YOU DO THAT*

Keeping communication channels open and
sending the right signals.

*Obi-Wan Kenobi, *Attack of the Clones*

Peter and Meredith Quill teach us:

SHARING YOUR LIFE'S SOUNDTRACK WITH YOUR KIDS IS AWESOME.

I t is often said that children are like sponges. At birth, most of the brain's one hundred billion neurons are not yet connected. But as children grow and learn, those connections are formed and reinforced at an astonishing rate. Everything we share helps shape who they are and becomes a part of our family's common culture. The movies we watch, the books we read, the expressions we use, and the music we listen to: kids soak it all up, reflect it back, and it's all woven into our collective memories and stories.

Peter Quill, the "Star-Lord" of the *Guardians of the Galaxy* 2014 film, knows just how important that kind of familial interconnection is. For twenty-six years in space, the only connection Quill has with his family or home planet is the

"Awesome Mix" tape of his mother Meredith's favorite pop songs from the 1960s and '70s. The night she died, Peter was abducted from Earth by space pirates; that selection of music is his only link to the world

he left behind. Peter calls upon the soundtrack throughout the film, from dancing to Redbone's "Come and Get Your Love" among the ruins of Morag to challenging his enemy Ronan to a dance-off while singing the Five Stairsteps' "O-o-h Child."

Peter risks his life to recover the old Sony Walkman his mom's mix tape lives in. When his companion Gamora asks him why, he explains that the device is for listening to music and dancing. Gamora scoffs, prompting Peter to recount the plot of a famous eighties movie as a fable: "On my planet, there's a legend about people like you. It's called *Footloose*. And in it, a great hero named Kevin Bacon teaches an entire city full of people with sticks up their butts that dancing—well, it's the greatest thing there is."

When Gamora finally gets Peter's point—"We're just like Kevin Bacon"—she shows how the *Footloose* story has become part of their little group's common culture. Which is to say: when we take the time to share our favorite cultural touchstones with our children, we reveal some of what shaped who we are. They won't realize it right away, and there will likely be lots of eye-rolling. Yet they can't help but absorb some of our faves and mix them into their own ongoing soundtrack. That's what heritage is all about.

AT LEAST FRICKIN' LISTEN TO THEM, OKAY?

P oking fun at the flicks of the 1960s, the *Austin Powers* action-comedies revolve around the relationship between the titular secret agent (played by Mike Myers) and his nemesis Dr. Evil (also played by Mike Myers). Both are revived in the modern day after having been cryogenically frozen, and their respective goals are simple: Dr. Evil wants to take over the world; Austin wants to stop him. Unfortunately, after three decades of cryosleep, their tactics and attitudes are more than a little outdated. The generation gap is highlighted in the films' other key relationship: the one between Dr. Evil and his son Scott. Scott desperately seeks his father's approval with every villainous scheme they look to hatch, even as he's filled with resentment at growing up with an absent, freeze-dried dad. For his part, Dr. Evil makes halfhearted attempts to bond with his son but gives up when he decides that Scott—who offers practical suggestions for dealing with Austin Powers, like "Why don't you just kill him?"—is, well, *just not evil enough.*

As parents, we spend a lot of our time talking to our kids: answering questions, teaching them life skills and manners, sharing hard-earned lessons. But kids aren't only passive receivers of information. Sometimes we need to stop lecturing and listen to what they're saying. Just look at Dr. Evil, so determined to tell his son exactly how to behave that he dismisses the child in front of him and clones himself a new one, Mini-Me. He misses out on the good ideas Scott is eager to offer. (Ideas like: "Don't call your deadly new secret weapon 'Preparation H,' because that's a thing already.")

Our kids want desperately for us to see and hear them. If we consider their suggestions, we teach them that their opinions have value. We show that even if we don't agree, we still respect them enough to reflect on what they say.

The truth is, the world is changing quickly, and—like it or not—our kids are often tapped into those changes more than we are. Scott mocks his father's goofy plans because, having actually lived through the past two decades, he can recognize Dr. Evil's redundancy. When we take the time to really listen to our kids, they usually teach us something. If not about the world, then at least about the unique individuals they are growing into.

The Cylons and the Final Five teach us:

BE SURE TO HAVE "THE TALK" BEFORE STUFF GETS CATACLYSMIC.

t starts with small signs of change—in their bodies, in their feelings. They begin to notice things that were once unimportant. They pay attention to people in a different way and may try on new personality traits. They may be compelled to act out, overwhelmed by urges, or overcome by powerful dreams.

When the seven models of humanoid Cylons from the rebooted *Battlestar Galactica* series begin to wake from their sleeper-agent states, it is a kind of adolescence. Everything they believe is called into question, and they have to rethink their identities and their allegiances. Our children are not humanoid cybernetic life forms—not unless their evolved hybrid progeny are reading this book in the far future, in which case, hi!—but they will still ask themselves many of the same kinds of questions as they grow up and move toward sexual maturity. Who am I? Where did I come from? Whom do I love? Why am I here?

Whether you're a newly awakened artificial life form or a prepubescent tween, there's a multifaceted discussion to be had, one involving biology, mechanics, physical development, contraception, emotions, body image, gender, relationships. Some of us will be more comfortable with certain aspects of "the talk" and less comfortable with others; there's no shame in consulting experts for help. But though we may not have all the answers, the important thing is to create an atmosphere that lets kids feel comfortable asking the questions. Keep in mind that the talk is really more like an ongoing conversation—one that evolves as our children mature.

Otherwise, things can go distressingly astray, as the "Final Five" Cylons, the millennia-old creator-parents of the other seven models, learn all too well. At the time of the fall of the Twelve Colonies, they, too, have had their memories suppressed and are unable to parent their progeny. Parents and children are helpless to assist one another as they slowly begin to remember; they turn to their peers to try to piece together their origins and future, falling prey along the way to much confusion and misinformation. Perhaps if the Final Five had been able to help nurture the Seven when it mattered, the Cylons would never have set out to destroy humanity.

We owe it to our children to give them the information they need—about sex, about the world at large—to make responsible choices for their future.

Akio, Yūko, and Chihiro Ogino teach us:

WHEN THE KIDS ARE EAGER TO SPIRIT YOU AWAY FROM BAD HABITS, PAY ATTENTION.

n the beginning of Hayao Miyazaki's 2001 animated film *Spirited Away*, ten-year-old Chihiro and her parents accidentally cross into the spirit world on their way to a new home. Seeing piles of food in an empty food-monger's stall, they devour a feast meant for the spirits. Chihiro refuses to join them, sensing that something is not quite right. Her parents ignore her protests and are transformed into pigs as punishment for their gluttony.

Kids can be pretty vocal when expressing concerns about parental vices and bad habits. Our children are protective of our health and well-being, and they're not shy about pointing out our harmful activities. Chihiro has a feeling that her family shouldn't stop at the seemingly abandoned amusement park or consume the food there. Her parents dismiss her concerns, and their subsequent transformation reflects not just their lack of self-control but their disregard for her opinions. In fact, in the throes of consumption, her mother and father cease caring about anything else and completely ignore Chihiro.

Just because our kids are young and inexperienced doesn't mean they aren't seeing us clearly. They witness patterns in our behavior that even we are unaware of. Fortunately, Chihiro perseveres through a series of trials, saves her parents, and finds a way to escape the trap her family walked into. The story reveals there's no harm in admitting that sometimes our kids are right—in fact, doing so can save us a lot of grief. We never want to put our children in the position of having to police our behavior. But sometimes their observations or questions may be exactly what we need to hear.

Anakin Skywalker and Obi-Wan Kenobi teach us:

IF YOU ALWAYS HARP ON WHAT THEY'RE DOING WRONG, YOU'RE TEACHING THEM TO FOCUS ON THE DARK SIDE.

More than any other adult, Obi-Wan Kenobi is the one who raised Anakin Skywalker from childhood. We know how much the Jedi Master cares for his young Padawan. But listen to Obi-Wan's conversations with the adolescent Anakin in the 2002 film *Attack of the Clones*, and you start to wonder. Pretty much every scene they share is full of negative reinforcement on the part of Obi-Wan. After the two meet Padmé: "Be mindful of your thoughts, Anakin. They'll betray you." When Anakin rescues his Master in a daring midair maneuver: "What took you so long?" When the teenager tries to lighten the mood with a joke: "If you spent as much time practicing your saber techniques as you did your wit . . . " Riding shotgun while Anakin pilots a speeder with Force-fueled mania: "You know I don't like it when you do that." And to top it all off, when Anakin calls him the "closest thing I have to a father," all Kenobi offers in response is: "Then why don't you listen to me?"

Discipline is vital. Kids—not just Jedi Padawans—need to develop the skills of self-control if they're one day to relate constructively to the rest of the world. It's a parent's job to help grow that self-control. To do so, you need a behavioral feedback structure that explicitly rewards accomplishment, à la the old idiom of the carrot and the stick. If your child's behavior seems to be prompting a lot of stick, take a deep breath, step back, and look for something they're doing that deserves the carrot. You know the competing philosophy: "The beatings will continue until morale improves"? It makes for a funny sign to hang on a pirate ship, but it doesn't do much for kids except make them distrust you.

The Jedi order's rejection of personal love as a distraction from a commitment to communal service is arguably part of what leads to their doom. If Anakin knew more clearly, more deeply, that his mentor really loved him, would it have helped him keep Obi-Wan closer in his heart, rather than letting Palpatine's dark-side manipulations sneak in through the cracks? Maybe. Remember that point when it's time to discipline kids. Yes, they need your tough love. But the tough only works if they're clear on the love.

MAKE SURE THEY KNOW TO PHONE HOME. AND MAKE SURE YOU'RE LISTENING WHEN THEY CALL.

When a spaceship carrying extraterrestrial explorers leaves behind one of their own, it's a lonely boy named Elliot who eventually befriends the gentle alien. The challenge for Elliot, and his brother and sister, is twofold. How can they communicate with E.T., and how can they help him get home?

Communication is at heart of our connections with other people. All day long, we send and receive messages: nonverbal cues, spoken words, written notes, texts. We shape our relationships and build our lives on those exchanges of information. But what happens when the person we're talking to isn't there—or isn't listening?

The three kids in Steven Spielberg's 1982 film *E.T. the Extra-Terrestrial* live with their mother, Mary Tyler. One of the earliest portrayals of a divorced mom in a family film, Mary is often frazzled as she tries to balance work and family, but nevertheless she's present in her kids' lives. In fact, for the first half of the movie she's the only adult whose face is shown. At one point early on, Mary suggests that Elliot call

his father, but Elliot replies that he can't because his father is in Mexico. His sadness at being unable to contact his out-of-the-country dad is later echoed by E.T., desperate to reconnect with his people some unknown billions of miles away.

E.T. is a film about friendship and communication. One of the phrases the precocious and adorable alien quickly learns is "Phone home." E.T. adapts a Speak & Spell toy and is able to send a distress call. But will it reach anyone? Thankfully, E.T.'s message is received. As the two friends say goodbye, E.T. touches his finger to Elliot's forehead and speaks the famous promise, "I'll be right here."

If E.T.'s call had gone to voicemail, or been dropped, or if nobody had picked up, the film would have had a very different ending. It reminds us that communication is a two-way street: both parties must be present to connect. We can give our kids cell phones to call us if they're in trouble; we can use Skype and FaceTime to keep in touch when we're away (these days, Elliot's dad would not be able to use a trip to Mexico as an excuse for being out of reach). But it's just as important to put down our phones during dinner so that our little aliens can talk to us face-to-face.

Fat Charlie and Mr. Nancy teach us:

THERE IS NO DAD, HOWEVER GODLIKE, WHO CAN RESIST OCCASIONALLY EMBARRASSING HIS KIDS IN PUBLIC.

Why does our culture so eagerly smile at the goofiness of dads, at their haplessness? Why is it that we praise high-achieving supermoms, yet celebrate the sheer mundanity of average-Joe fatherhood? Just in the past decade, the concepts of the "dad joke" and the "dad bod"—both lionized for their comfortable mediocrity—have arrived front and center in the popular discussion of dadhood. (Meanwhile, a common mom-related slang phrase of the same era is, shall we say, decidedly less polite.) Here's one possible answer: our societal vision of masculinity is all wrapped up in power and authority. Knowing just how toxic that masculine identity can be, we instinctively go out of our way to laud fatherly traits that we hope undermine the idea of tyranny. Like having a body that's not particularly threatening. Like making terrible but harmless jokes, and laughing hysterically at them.

In Neil Gaiman's 2005 novel *Anansi Boys*, Mr. Nancy is the elderly, eternally amused father of the mild-mannered white-collar Londoner "Fat Charlie" Nancy. Unbeknownst to his son, he's also an incarnation of the African trickster god Anansi. Mr. Nancy generally tries to keep the impact of his divine will benevolent. Mostly this means mortifying his kid by dancing, singing, and otherwise acting in ways that embarrass

Fat Charlie but that everyone else finds perfectly charming.

Traditionally, goofy humor has been one of a relative few forms of behavior that can be gentle while still deemed "manly." It's a shame that, even in the twenty-first century, we have so few culturally acceptable expressions of masculine emotion. When boys and men are routinely praised for being gentle and encouraged to be kind, what we'll get is a more compassionate world.

Meanwhile, parents in general, and perhaps dads in particular, should heed the fine line that separates harmless teasing from unintentional cruelty. It's Mr. Nancy, for instance, who glibly dubbed his son "Fat" Charlie, an unwanted nickname. Overcoming his subtle dissatisfaction with his own state of being turned out to be a lifelong struggle—one that left Charlie pursuing the wrong sort of career and engaged to the wrong sort of person (for him).

Humor should be liberating, not oppressive. At their best, dad jokes have a certain amount of self-mockery that brings the booming-voiced patriarch down to the level of just another goofy kid. And it's at that level, through all the groans and eye rolls, that we have the opportunity to really connect with our kids. Just be sure that the joke's not on them.

Deanna and Lwaxana Troi teach us:

EVEN IF YOU CAN READ MINDS, MEDDLING IN YOUR CHILD'S LOVE LIFE IS A WAY TO FEEL GREAT PAIN.

waxana Troi, a recurring character in *Star Trek: The Next Generation*, is a woman who knows what she wants and stops at nothing to get it. So she cannot understand why her daughter, Counselor Deanna Troi, is so uptight, particularly when it comes to men. As the Betazoid Federation ambassador, daughter of the Fifth House of Betazed, holder of the Sacred Chalice of Rixx, and heir to the Holy Rings of Betazed, Lwaxana is powerful and privileged enough to have moved beyond caring what other people think. Especially since, being a telepath, she knows exactly what most of them *are* thinking.

We want our children to be happy and find love, but our view of dating and marriage may not be the same as theirs. Lwaxana eagerly elicits and relishes the attention of many potential lovers, much to the chagrin of her more conservative daughter. In her position of authority on the USS *Enterprise*, Deanna is well respected by the crew for being both poised and sensitive. Her focus is on her career and the needs of the ship.

Fortunately, communication is important for both mother and daughter, and over time each learns from the other. Deanna helps her mother work through long-suppressed grief, and Lwaxana helps her daughter open up to love. Even though Lwaxana may never fully understand that for Deanna, following Captain Picard's orders on the bridge is as valid a priority as giving orders to Commander Riker in the bedroom.

Unlike Lwaxana, we can't read our kids' minds. If we really want to know what they're thinking, we have to ask them. And then wait until they're ready to tell us.

THE CRICKET ON YOUR KID'S SHOULDER HAS TO SAY MORE THAN "BECAUSE I SAID SO."

onsider kindhearted Geppetto, who lives in a cottage full of handmade clocks, music boxes, and wood-carved toys. He dreams of a child of his own, and so he creates a marionette out of pine that he names Pinocchio. That night, the Blue Fairy grants his wish and brings the marionette to life. And here's where the Disney animated film dramatically diverges from the original Carlo Collodi story, which is a cautionary tale that ends in tragedy. The Disney version features a more innocent Pinocchio, a puppet who is promised that he can become a real boy if he is "brave, truthful, and unselfish."

But how is a newly created wooden child supposed to learn about integrity? He needs a conscience, of course. Fortunately, Pinocchio gets one in the form of Jiminy Cricket, a drifter assigned by the Blue Fairy to be "Lord high keeper of the knowledge of right and wrong, counselor in moments of temptation, and guide along the straight and narrow path."

Jiminy stumbles, however, because he tries to help

Pinocchio by telling the boy what to do, but fails to provide context or explanation. When Pinocchio is lured by the so-called Honest John to pursue a life on the stage, Jiminy tells Pinocchio he must go to school instead. Pinocchio initially agrees with Jiminy, but he doesn't really understand *why*. So he goes with Honest John and lies about it to the Blue Fairy. Just like all kids, wooden or real, Pinocchio will learn that his actions have consequences. Since the cricket didn't attempt to explain himself, this revelatory moment is played out when a curse transforms Pinocchio and his friends into literal jackasses because of their mischief.

When we say anything along the lines of "Because I said so," we're wielding our authority as an exclamation point to end the conversation—and the learning. It may sometimes be necessary, but as a default response, it doesn't empower our kids to make good choices. Not only that, also it makes them feel helpless.

Kids get upset when their wishes are denied, even if we give them a thoughtful "No." They will try to wear us down with repeated demands. But what matters is that, over time, they internalize *why* we said no. The process is slower than a magical curse, but the results are long lasting—and thoroughly real.

BREAKING A PINKY PROMISE CAN HAVE DESPICABLE CONSEQUENCES.

Hoping to become the world's greatest villain, *Despicable Me*'s Felonius Gru has a plan to shrink and steal the moon. To do so, he needs the assistance of three cookie-delivering little girls to help him gain access to the home of his nemesis, Vector. Under the pretense of looking for children to adopt, Gru goes to Miss Hattie's Home for Girls and brings home the orphaned Margo, Edith, and Agnes to assist him in pulling off the heist of the century. Gru intends to borrow the girls for a few days, long enough to steal Vector's shrink ray. But it takes only that much time for the girls turn his life (and his lair) upside down, adding crayon drawings and lace into his medieval chic decor and generally softening his heart as they weave themselves into his life.

Children instinctively trust their parents—we take care of them, we love them, and they believe us when we tell them something. Words have power, and children take promises seriously. Gru may only half-heartedly "pinky swear" to little Agnes when she asks if he will attend the girls' dance recital, but the girls take his promise to heart. He sends them back to Miss Hattie's and moves forward with his plan to steal the moon rather than go to their show. Still, the girls still hold on to the hope that he'll come and even make a sign to decorate his saved seat in the auditorium. When Gru tries to make it to the performance after stealing the moon, he's too late. Not only does he miss the show, but his absence also makes it possible for Vector to kidnap the girls.

When we break a promise to our kids, we make them feel less important than whatever it was that took away our time and attention. And the more promises we break, the harder it is to regain their trust.

For the girls, Gru's desire to become the greatest villain of all time seems stronger than his love for them. But ultimately Gru gives up the moon, adopts the girls, and strives to recover their trust as a committed father. That's a good example for us to follow, along with apologies, explanation, and promises to do better. Because, even when what's at stake isn't literally the moon, our kids' expectations can loom just as large—and our actions exert just as strong a gravitational pull on their hearts.

Chakotay and Kolopak teach us:

TRADITION IS MORE THAN SKIN DEEP.

When *Star Trek: Voyager*'s Commander Chakotay was young, he refused the forehead tattoo of his people, just as he rejected many of the traditions it represented. Unlike his father, Kolopak, who believed strongly in their heritage, Chakotay was more interested in reaching for the stars rather than stretching to the past. He refused to etch such a prominent and permanent symbol on his body just because it was expected.

Many cultures have outward manifestations of their traditions and beliefs: the turbans worn by Sikh men, the long beards of Hasidic Jews, the hijab donned by some Muslim women. These are powerful, intentional statements of one's identity even if a community is insular and those adornments are the norm. All the more so when people from different cultures mix. Chakotay wishes not to be connected to the traditions of his people by adopting a symbol that represents beliefs he has rejected.

Most parents with concerns about tattoos and similar body adornment worry about their kids wanting, not rejecting, such decorations. Nevertheless, Kolopak's disappointment resonates. He wanted to teach his son the importance of the old myths and the old ways. Similarly, we may feel that our child's tattoo or piercing is a rejection of the values we've tried to teach.

Whether they're resisting a tradition we consider sacrosanct or making choices about their appearance that we consider ill-advised, it's helpful to ask our kids about their motivation. If our children talk to us about dyeing their hair, putting on a burka, or getting a tattoo, the first thing we should do is listen. A knee-jerk "No!"—even if that's our honest reaction—will only push them away. A conversation enables discussion about respecting cultural history and the fleeting nature of likes and dislikes. We can ask thought-provoking questions as well as raise practical concerns (like the safety of the tattoo parlor or the skill of a specific artist).

After his father's death, Chakotay chooses to mark his forehead with the tribal tattoo of his people. On his own terms, in his own time, he comes to embrace the symbol that connects him with his father and his Native American heritage. Perhaps talking with us will convince our kids they're not really ready for whatever commitment gives us pause. Or perhaps we'll come to understand just how important that indelible ink is to their identity. Either way, the result will hopefully be for the best.

Hiro and Kaito Nakamura teach us:

CHILDREN FIND THEIR OWN HEROES.

I n 2006, the TV show *Heroes* introduced a young generation of new superheroes struggling to deal with their powers. More than just a group of mutant misfits working together, *Heroes* is a multigenerational story of children dealing with the events set into motion by their superhero parents. Take the homophonous Hiro Nakamura: ever since he was a boy, he's aspired to save the day, drawing inspiration from far-out epic stories and comic books. Hiro views the world and his powers through the lens of science fiction, adopting its language in philosophy and practice. He frequently offers Spock's Vulcan hand salute ("Live long and prosper") and has developed his own set of rules, such as: "Every hero must learn his purpose."

Hiro's father, Kaito Nakamura, is one of the older generation of heroes. A brilliant businessman and savvy swordsman, Kaito has little hope that his son's comic books and idealism will ever translate into real-world heroism. For Kaito, a "real" hero is the legendary warrior Takezo Kenzei. As it turns out, in *Heroes*, comics literally help prevent the end of the world. Specifically, a comic called *9th Wonders!,* whose artist has the power to foretell the future and whose artwork is invaluable in helping Hiro and his fellow heroes succeed in their quest.

Despite our best intentions, even Earth's mightiest parents

cannot be the sole source of wisdom in our children's lives. They'll seek sagacity from other sources, not all of which will be familiar, or even comprehensible, to us. Unlike Hiro's father, we geek parents would be thrilled to see our children inspired by comic books. But what if, in typical child-rebel fashion, your kid eschews comics in favor of something more mundane? What if your Hiro develops rules based on the *Wall Street Journal* or *Transit Maps of the World*?

Our kids' cultural touchstones are just as valid as ours—jazz leads to rock leads to hip-hop and so on. To think otherwise is to be blinded by our own hubris. The pragmatic Kaito tries to anticipate his son's needs. But Hiro doesn't want to follow in his father's entrepreneurial footsteps. After watching from afar as his son applies the otherworldly lessons he has learned, Kaito comes to respect Hiro's worldview. "For close to thirty years, I have seen my son as a disappointment," he admits. "A dreamer who excelled at nothing. It was not until Hiro began this quest that I saw his strength, courage, and wisdom."

The wise parent realizes there are as many different kinds of heroes as there are legends, books, movies, and comics to find them in. As long as our children are inspired to do well—and do good—it doesn't matter whose myths inspire them.

Jacob and Ronald Taylor teach us:

NO MATTER HOW FAR YOU RUN—EVEN TO THE FAR END OF THE MILKY WAY— UNFINISHED FAMILY BUSINESS DEMANDS TO BE TAKEN CARE OF.

ormer space marine and biotic-powered warrior Jacob Taylor never knew what became of his father, Ronald, first officer on the starship *Hugo Gernsback*, which vanished in deep space a decade earlier. So when a distress beacon from the *Gernsback* is detected, there's not much question: the moment Jacob's current mission is over, he will convince his squad leader Commander Shepard to cross the galaxy so that they can investigate the mysterious signal.

Mysteries about our families, about our personal origins, usually aren't something we can let stand quietly forever. Adopted kids will wonder about birth parents, no matter how much they love and appreciate the parents who raised them. Uncles or aunts or grandparents who fall off the map and are never heard from again remain a big fat question mark until the next generation finds a way to turn them into a period.

The Mass Effect video game reveals that after Ronald Taylor's ship crashed, he went all *Heart of Darkness*, spending years inflicting his violent power fantasies upon the other survivors. It's a discovery that Jacob's horrified to make. Yet even so, knowing is somehow more satisfying than spending the rest of his life wondering if and why his father had abandoned him.

Life can be messy, and sometimes we think our kids would be better off not knowing about the aspects of our lives that we're not proud of. But an intimate question mark, and the associated fear and shame that leaves kids wondering if *they* did something wrong, can become a wound that doesn't heal properly until it's treated with a dose of truth. Apply the necessary medicine so that everyone can move forward.

Orpheus and Morpheus teach us:

FAMILY GRUDGES WILL TURN ENDLESS IF YOU LET THEM.

In life, as in fiction, parents and kids sometimes say hurtful, devastating things to each other; tempers flare, families fracture. The more powerful the family, it seems, the greater the potential for dysfunction. We see this in the interaction of the immortal siblings known as the Endless—Dream (a.k.a. Morpheus), Destruction, Death, Desire, Delirium, Despair, and Destiny—chronicled in Neil Gaiman's comic *The Sandman*.

In *The Sandman*'s version of classic Greek mythology, the bard Orpheus is the only child of Dream and Calliope, the muse of epic poetry. Orpheus marries his beloved Euridice, only to have her die from a viper bite on their wedding night. Orpheus cries out for his father, who answers him coolly: "She is dead. You are alive. So live." Although true, Dream's words bring little comfort. Orpheus rejects both his father and his advice, turning instead to the godlike powers of his aunt (who happens to be Death) and uncle (Destruction) to help him march into the underworld and undo his bride's demise. He still fails, however. Devastated, Orpheus allows his body to be torn to pieces by the mad Bacchante. But because of the deal with Death he'd just made while trying to save Euridice, Orpheus is doomed to remain alive eternally, as a disembodied head sadly crying out his beloved's name.

Dream comes to Orpheus, but only to promise his son that he will never see him again. Stubborn and proud, Dream can't admit the pain it causes him to see his son's life ruined forever because Orpheus didn't heed his wisdom. As a defense mechanism, he rejects his child. Both are essentially immortal, and forever is a very long time to hold a grudge.

Letting go of strong emotions isn't easy, but we must consider the cost of holding on to those feelings. When we nurture a grudge against our kids, we trap ourselves and our children in that resentment—just like Orpheus's head stuck in the sand on a distant beach, weeping alone. We don't have to endorse decisions we consider ill-advised, but that doesn't mean we should go the Morpheus route, punishing our kids by withholding our love. Morpheus came around eventually, but only centuries later, when he needed Orpheus's oracular vision. Most of us won't have that kind of time.

LET THEM KNOW YOU'LL STILL LOVE THEM EVEN IF THEY REVEAL THEIR SECRET IDENTITY.

For the first thirty-nine issues of the Amazing Spider-Man comic, Peter Parker's Aunt May had no idea her nephew led a secret life as a web-slinging, crime-fighting superhero. In fact, she frequently voiced intense and opposite feelings for the two sides of Peter's double identity. Her nephew was the light of her life, a hardworking young man she'd raised from orphanhood to become the kindhearted model citizen she so adored. But "that horrible Spider-Man" was, as the tabloid news media assured her, a dangerous menace, an out-of-control freak who put regular folks' lives at risk.

Aunt May's inability to see through the fog of ignorance and fear-mongering propaganda—her failure to recognize her own kin's good soul and humanity underneath the outlandishly garish outfit in which Spider-Man swung around the city—added no end of stress, heartache, and self-hatred to Peter's adolescence. He felt awful lying to her, keeping such a profound life-sized secret from his closest family. Why could his aunt not grasp that the superhero's unconventional identity was a choice to do good with the power he'd been given, not a defiant act of rebellion?

Aunt May just didn't get it—until, finally, one fateful day well into Peter's adult life, she entered his apartment to find him asleep, freshly bloodied from battling a supervillain, still half-dressed in his Spider-Man costume. Shocked and confused, she spent the next days relentlessly searching the Internet, looking up every fact about the masked vigilante that she could find, slowly realizing that she'd been blind to all the good he'd been doing all those years, all the lives he'd been saving.

Most teenagers with a secret identity aren't superpowered crime-fighters. But their secrets can be equally burdensome, if not more so. Maybe they're LGBT people who don't know how to come out to their loved ones. Maybe they're struggling with addiction or body-image issues. Whatever the reason, fearing that your friends and families will despise your truth is a painful and soul-crushing ordeal. Don't risk putting your kids through it. Make clear to them early and often that, whatever their path in life, you'll always love them. Because they're your kids; because you're their parents. Compared to that fact, what they wear at night and how they swing are small details, indeed.

Victor, Edward, and Susan Frankenstein teach us:

WHEN IT'S A MATTER OF LIFE AND DEATH, SAVE THE LECTURE FOR LATER.

In Tim Burton's 2012 film *Frankenweenie,* Edward and Susan Frankenstein are supportive of their quirky and brilliant son Victor. They encourage his passion for science and filmmaking, but still express concern about his alienation. When his beloved dog Sparky is killed by a passing car, Victor is devastated. "When you lose someone you love, they never really leave you," his mother says, trying to comfort her son. "They just move into a special place in your heart. If we could bring him back, we would."

A lecture on electricity by his science teacher, Mr. Rzykruski, inspires Victor to do just that: to bring back Sparky with a little help from love and lightning. Much to Victor's delight, his best friend returns as the same sweet dog he always was (except for some stitching and the need for occasional recharging). When Victor's parents discover the reanimated animal in the attic, however, their fear sends Sparky

fleeing from the house, a panicked Victor following after him. His parents want to talk with Victor about the ethics of what he's done. "Reanimating a corpse," his father says, "it's very—" And then he pauses, thinking carefully about which word to choose next. He finishes with "upsetting."

Victor's father could have chosen different words: wrong, stupid, naive, erroneous. Instead he picks a word that doesn't condemn or judge his son. He does so because Edward and Susan recognize Victor's immediate heartache. "Sweetheart, we'll help you look for Sparky," his mother says, "but when we get back, I think we have to have a little talk. Understood?"

Our kids will upset us; they are going to make choices we don't agree with. The lesson is to stop and think before we respond. To lecture Victor about the repercussions of reanimation while his dog is still in danger would have been cruel—and Victor would not have been in a receptive state to take those messages to heart. Children do need to learn about consequences, to have conversations with us about choices and ethics. But there's a time and place for that dialogue. Sometimes, as in Victor and Sparky's case, we'll find that no lecture is needed. The natural consequences of their actions will teach our children the most valuable lessons.

4

~~~~~~~~~~~~~~~~~

EXPECTO PATRONUM!*

Keeping them safe.

THE WORLD IS FULL OF MONSTERS. MAKE SURE YOUR KIDS KNOW WHAT THEY LOOK LIKE.

iven the chance, the evil creatures lurking in the shadows on the TV show *Supernatural* will absolutely hurt children. It's a world in which angelic and demonic forces frequently interfere in the events of women and men, using humanity as pawns or fodder. After the demon Azazel brutally murders John Winchester's wife, the grieving widower devotes his life to hunting those monsters while trying to keep his sons, Dean and Sam, safe. John is arguably not as present in his boys' lives as he might be. In fact, he leaves them alone for weeks at a time as he goes off in pursuit of ghosts, demons, and other creatures. But he does his best to make his sons aware of the evil that exists in the world and to equip them with the knowledge they need to stand strong against it.

Monsters are real. Kids already know this. That's why they can't resist the allure of being *safely* scared; it's why children's stories are full of power-hungry wizards and murderous queens, bloodthirsty vampires and ghastly ghouls. In his essay "The Red Angel," G. K. Chesterton make this brilliant point, often cited in discussion of scary stories and children: "Fairy tales do not give the child his first idea of bogey. What fairy tales give the child is his first clear idea of the possible defeat of bogey. The baby has known the dragon intimately ever since he had an imagination. What the fairy tale provides for him is a St. George to kill the dragon."

To see the monsters of our world, we need only read or watch the news. We can help our children learn to identify these violent threats by explaining the world to them honestly, little by little, to the degree that they can understand. Along with the ogres and the dragons, we can show them heroes, too. Not just fictional ones like the Winchester brothers, but real-life heroes, from a neighbor who volunteers at a homeless shelter to icons of heroism like Malala Yousafzai. One day our children will take their turn standing up against the monsters, and we want them to be ready.

Roy Neary and his family teach us:

TAKE THE MASHED POTATOES SERIOUSLY.

oy Neary doesn't know exactly what it is that's haunting him. He knows that he saw an unidentified flying object. But the strange mountain-like shape keeps flickering in his mind's eye, and he has no idea what that is. Desperate to figure it out, he keeps trying to re-create the image in three-dimensional reality—as a sculpture of mud, as a blob of shaving cream, out of the heaping helping of mashed potatoes on his dinner plate. The obsession leads his wife to lose faith in his sanity and his marital commitment. She leaves him, taking their kids with her.

Roy's not uncommitted to his family. He's just trying as best he can to deal with a huge revelation about life that he never imagined he'd have to face. In the 1977 Steven Spielberg film *Close Encounters of the Third Kind*, that revelation is the existence of alien life in the universe. But in our everyday lives, we're often thrown off our axis by more personal bombshells. Maybe there's a long-lost relative we never knew about. Maybe our spouse hasn't been sharing a financial problem with us. Or maybe someone has been mistreating a child when no responsible adults have been paying attention.

As a parent, you have to trust your gut. That doesn't mean being hasty or irrational—it means that, when your senses are screaming at you that something isn't right, you need to take that feeling seriously and examine the situation carefully. In Roy's case, he used whatever materials were at hand. Which, let's admit, did make him seem less than rational. The important thing is that he wasn't satisfied until he found out what triggered the alarm bells. (Turned out to be an alien mothership at the top of Devil's Tower in Wyoming. NBD.) Like Roy, we need to be persistent when trying to get at the truth of a problem that worries us. Plenty of things going on in the world theoretically *should* be fine, people will assure you they are fine, but that nonetheless they are not really fine.

When these sorts of things bump up against your family, you may need to climb a metaphorical mountain to get a close encounter with the answers you need.

SLUMBERLAND CAN BE A SCARY PLACE. BE THERE WHEN THEY WAKE UP.

When it first appeared in the *New York Herald* in 1905, the comic strip *Little Nemo in Slumberland* introduced readers to the beautiful and sometimes frightening dream vistas of one boy, Little Nemo. Most comic artists of the time focused on characters, but Winsor McCay sketched the architecture and landscapes of Slumberland with a level of detail and scale never before seen in newspaper strips.

In McCay's stories, Nemo's waking life is rarely portrayed except for the ending panel. Nearly every weekly strip concludes with Nemo falling out of bed or being woken from a fitful slumber by one of his parents. His mother and father usually chastise their son for making a ruckus in his sleep or for questionable nighttime snacking that likely caused the nightmare. (Turkey dressing, raw onions, and ice cream . . .) The important thing is that, after Nemo's vivid night of spinning around on Saturn's rings or being turned into a monkey, his parents are always there to ground him in the real world once again.

Each time Nemo falls asleep, he travels deeper through Slumberland. Ultimately, he learns enough to be able to lucid-dream and remain conscious. In other words, he gains the tools necessary to control his environment, which is an important ability for people to feel capable of basic functioning. Sometimes kids who have a lot of nightmares become fearful of falling asleep; for those who suffer from even stronger phenomena like sleep paralysis, issues around sleep can become an emotional drain on waking life. Some kids just go through a stage when peacefully drifting off to dreamland isn't in their nature. Regardless of the underlying causes, we can provide our children with both strategies and gear that can help them feel more in control, whether it's a nightlight, bedtime routines, protective stuffed animals, dreamcatchers, or breathing techniques. And, like Nemo's parents, we can make sure that our frustration with their sleeping habits doesn't mean we won't tuck them in every time.

Akin to Santa Claus or the tooth fairy, dreams have no physical existence. Yet they can loom just as large in kids' interior reality as any person, place, or thing they know from the tangible world. For both good and ill, dreams can affect their lives in a way that's too real to dismiss. Remembering that can help us mediate the awful nighttime imaginings, even as we encourage them to chase the inspiring ones.

Veronica and Keith Mars teach us:

THE HERO
IS THE ONE WHO
STAYS.

Bad things happen. Sometimes a *lot* of bad things happen, all at once. The television series *Veronica Mars* begins with a slew of bad things happening: Veronica's best friend Lilly is murdered. Veronica's father, county sheriff Keith Mars, pursues Lilly's father as the main suspect. But Lilly's father, a wealthy pillar of the community, turns out to be innocent, and the false accusation gets Keith stripped of his position. The Mars family is stigmatized, Veronica loses her high school peer group, and she's drugged and raped at a party held by her former friends. Her alcoholic mother leaves suddenly under vague circumstances, her father's paternity is called into question—and the drama continues from there.

High school is hard enough without the overwhelming avalanche of misfortune that hits Veronica in the show's first few episodes. She and her father get through it with the other's help, and it is their relationship that forms the heart of the three-season mystery-of-the-week series. Assisting her father in his new job as a private investigator, Veronica displays impulsive, creative thinking that provides a counterbalance to Keith's steadfast moral compass. Veronica supports her father even when it costs her friends and her status, and when she twists the truth or takes dangerous risks, Keith stands by her.

At one point, Keith tells his daughter: "If I were in trouble, I'd want you on my side." Veronica answers: "Well, that's where I'd be." She has learned from her father that when times get tough, you don't run away. When bad things happen, heroes stay, whether they're facing vampires, killer robots, or the unfair vagaries of fate.

Mrs. Brisby and her children teach us:

WHEN A TIMID LITTLE MOUSE OF A SINGLE MOM NEEDS TO BE A HERO, SHE WILL BE. THAT'S WHAT MOMS DO.

The world can be a terrifying place, full of predators and natural disasters. And when we have little ones entrusted into our care, we do whatever we can to prevent tragedy. But sometimes it's unavoidable: One day, the cat is going to attack. One day, Farmer Fitzgibbon will decide to plow early. One day, the cinder-block home where your cheery little mouse family resides is going to sink into the mud.

Rarely do mothers have the adventure in stories—usually the children or the fathers are the ones who leave home to save the world. But in the dark and beautifully hand-animated film *The Secret of NIMH*, the widowed mouse Mrs. Brisby goes off in search of a solution to rescue her family's home from destruction. First she seeks out the neighboring community of cerebrally enhanced rats—friends of her late husband, Jonathan, who years ago escaped alongside them from horrific experiments at NIMH. (Yes, that's the National Institute of Mental Health, for those who keep up with *Psychology Today*.) The rats agree to use their advanced technology and super-intelligence to help Mrs. Brisby move her house out of the path of the plow. In doing so, they risk being discovered and recaptured; in the end it is Mrs. Brisby who saves the day, not only for her family but for all the rats involved, by drawing upon incredible bravery.

Sometimes the list of possible catastrophes that could endanger our kids seems endless. We can only do our best to prepare, trying not to obsess over imaginary hazards. But never forget: when offspring are threatened, the primal response of mothers, no matter the species, will transform even the gentlest of creatures into a ferocious protector.

Mrs. Brisby shows us that even an unassuming parent can become a hero. If an ordinary mouse can face down cats and fanatics, then we, too, must be capable of calling up extraordinary courage whenever our children need it.

Sarah and John Connor teach us:

IF YOUR CHILD DOESN'T FACE THOSE BULLIES, INSECURITIES, OR KILLER ROBOTS FROM THE FUTURE, THEY'LL BE BACK.

I f anyone has the motivation to be a helicopter parent, it's Sarah Connor. A single mother tasked with raising the boy who will eventually save humanity from the cyborgs, Sarah's entire life is devoted to serving as her son's protector and mentor. We may not face the specific stress of preparing our children to prevent the end of the world, but we do need to prepare them to face life's challenges as confident, self-sufficient adults. That means letting them face their battles when they're able to do so.

Of course there will be situations when even older children need the added weight of a parental voice or action. But that's not the same as stepping in and solving the problems that they should be able to handle on their own. Our kids don't need us to argue with their college professors over grades. They don't need us to go with them job interviews or negotiate their salaries. Micromanaging their lives doesn't help them be autonomous, resourceful adults.

In the movie franchise of that name, the first Terminator—the T-800—is sent by Skynet from the future to kill Sarah Connor. Its goal is to prevent John's conception and birth, which means Sarah's life is also on the line. With the help of John's father—also sent from the future—Sarah defeats the T-800 and gains the confidence she needs to raise a rebel leader. As John grows through early childhood, she teaches him to beware the killer machines at all costs, to battle them when they show up again. Good thing, too: when Skynet sends an upgraded model, the T-1000, Sarah is in a prison for the criminally insane, and a teenage John must decide what to do. Then he's confronted with a reprogrammed T-800, purportedly sent by his own future self to help. John opts to trust the T-800—and that choice, an approach his mother could not possibly have predicted or suggested, is what allows them to defeat the T-1000.

Our protective parental impulse is strong. But sometimes the best we can do is recognize when the moment of truth has come and trust our child to face a dilemma solo. John Connor does end up saving not only himself, but also the future. He does it because Sarah has prepared him sufficiently. Even though his mother becomes dehumanized in her quest to protect her son, John manages to hold fast to his humanity, and that is what ultimately protects them all. But he never could have done it had his mother not taught him to make sound decisions all on his own.

THERE'S A WORD FOR AN ADULT WHO TRIES TO SCARE A CHILD INTO KEEPING A SECRET: SUPERVILLAIN.

We all know that the original Spider-Man, Peter Parker, learned his central life lesson from his kindhearted Uncle Ben, an upstanding citizen who taught him that with great power comes great responsibility. As it turns out, the newest teenager in the Marvel Comics universe to pick up the mantle of Spider-Man, Miles Morales, learns something similar from his own uncle, but in a very different way.

Whereas Ben Parker was tragically murdered by a burglar whom Peter could have stopped earlier in the day if he'd been living up to his uncle's advice, Miles finds himself in a different moral quandary. His Uncle Aaron *is* a burglar and a murderer. In fact, he's secretly the masked supervillain called the Prowler. And when Aaron discovers his nephew is Spider-Man, he abuses the closeness of their relationship to try to emotionally, and then physically, intimidate Miles into becoming his partner—and keeping his secret.

That kind of intimidation is familiar to anyone who's had real-life experience with child abuse. A common first-person account of many abuse survivors is that, harmful as the physical assault is, the deepest trauma usually results from the intense pressure to hide and deny the truth of what happened. They fear being disbelieved, blamed, stigmatized.

But victims of abuse stand the best chance of healing if they know they can turn to people who will believe them, stand by them, and never ask them to keep a deep dark secret that eats at them forever. Which is why children need to hear, at a young age, that nobody is allowed to make them stay quiet about something that bothers them. And that anyone who tells them they *have* to keep quiet is lying and not to be trusted.

Doing the right thing frequently involves telling a hard truth. If our children need their truth to be heard, they need to know we'll be right there with them when they tell it.

SCISSORS AND OTHER TOOLS ARE MADE TO BE USED—AND RESPECTED.

Knives, hammers, scissors. These are tools that help us in our lives, but they can be dangerous when used incorrectly or with ill intention. And sometimes malicious intent is in the eye of the beholder, since people often fear what they don't understand. As, for example, when meeting a teenage boy with scissors in the place of hands. When Avon saleswoman Peg Boggs visits the home of a deceased inventor, she finds one of his creations, Edward, living all alone in the dark mansion on the hill. She's nervous until she talks with him, after which Peg immediately invites the young man home to live with her family. Edward introduces whimsy into her homogeneous suburban neighborhood. Not only does he stand out with his bladed appendages and goth-boy good looks, but he also has the soul and skill of an artist.

Oversized and sharp, Edward's scissor-hands are sometimes unwieldy. He accidentally hurts Peg's daughter Kim, with whom he has fallen in love. Despite his gentle spirit and ability to create breathtaking topiary, Edward is eventually ostracized by the townspeople. Much as in *Frankenstein* and other monster movies, the fearful masses cannot reconcile a beautiful spirit within a frightening exterior. Attacked by Kim's ex-boyfriend, Edward accidentally kills him in self-defense. He then fakes his own death and returns to a life of isolation—except for the occasional shaved ice that he causes to fall on the California town, a secret message to his beloved Kim.

The inventor who created Edward died before he was able to give the boy real hands. His scissors were never intended to be permanent, and so Edward was never really instructed on how to use them wisely around other people. He had no choice but to use them all the time, and for everything, pushing his prosthetic scissor-fingers far beyond the uses they were intended for. In that scenario, accidents are inevitable.

Whatever implements our children want to handle—carpentry tools, power tools, or the digital tools of web browser and smartphone—they'll be better off if we teach them the correct ways to use them. Supervising as they practice, rather than forbidding them from ever touching anything potentially dangerous, does require more effort on our part. But a child who learns to use tools properly—and safely—gains confidence and lifelong proficiency. And as we learn from Edward and Kim, ignorance and fear in the wrong hands can be far more dangerous than an innocent pair of scissors in the right ones.

Harry Potter and Remus Lupin teach us:

PROTECTING OUR CHILDREN INCLUDES TEACHING THEM TO PROTECT THEMSELVES.

In J. K. Rowling's Harry Potter series, one of the oldest and most advanced of the defensive spells is the Patronus Charm. Few are able to master the spell, which allows a wizard to conjure a magical guardian. The Patronus Charm requires the recollection of a wizard's happiest memory, accompanied by concentration and incantation. Harry is taught how to cast the powerful spell by Remus Lupin, one of Harry's late father's best friends. Remus, who naturally possesses paternal feelings toward his close friend's son, becomes one of Harry's most beloved professors at the Hogwarts school. Harry later teaches the Patronus Charm to his peers, allowing them all to defend against otherwise unstoppable Dementors.

If parents could employ magic to keep our children safe, we would be on the next train to Hogwarts. Unfortunately, we are Muggles and must resort to the mundane tools at our disposal. When they're little, keeping children safe is a simpler affair because they're with us so much of the time. The older they get, the more time they spend away from us. It's then that some of the most valuable protection we can offer is education about the things that can hurt them.

Of course, *protection* is a term many of us use as shorthand for "birth control and STD prevention." It's a topic that can be hard to speak about frankly, and some parents worry that talking about preventative measures will encourage kids to have sex. Studies have shown, however, that the opposite is true. When parents provide children with the facts about sex and discuss their values with them, they are more likely to delay that child's having sex—and to encourage the use of protection when they do.

The Patronus Charm was considered advanced magic, not usually taught to young wizards like Harry and his classmates. But if they hadn't learned it, they may not have survived the unexpected dangers that came upon them. It can be difficult to think that our kids are ready for the "sex talk," or other conversations about the risks awaiting them as they grow into adulthood. But, like the happiness-eating Dementors, many of the hazards our children will face seem to come out of nowhere. And putting off those frank, if uncomfortable, conversations could leave our kids unprotected when they're most in need of defense.

Sam and Michael Emerson and their grandfather teach us:

IF YOUR KIDS' FRIENDS ARE VAMPIRES, YOU'RE GONNA WANT TO KNOW THAT FACT AHEAD OF TIME.

When our children are young, we can plan playdates and parties. As they get older, we have less control; we cannot dictate whom they'll befriend, spend time with, or confide in. Still, we can and should do our best to get to know who those people are. We see this lesson at work in the seminal vampire tale of a generation: before Buffy's star-crossed slayer romance or the sexy Bayou bloodsuckers of *True Blood*, the 1987 film *The Lost Boys* gave us teenage angst along with the fishnets, shoulder pads, and bleached mullets of 1980s California.

After their parents' divorce, Sam and his older brother Michael move with their mother to the dying coastal town of Santa Carla to live with their grandfather, a quirky taxidermist. Michael becomes infatuated with Star, a beautiful runaway he sees on the boardwalk, and he quickly joins a rowdy gang of teenagers in an effort to get to know her better. Turns out the homeless teens aren't just delinquents and drifters—they're vampires who make their home in underground caverns and prey upon visitors to the town's boardwalk and beaches. Meanwhile, Sam befriends the Frog brothers in their local comic book shop. These two self-appointed vampire hunters recruit Sam to help them rid the town of its bloodsucking affliction—but not before Sam's brother Michael is tricked into drinking vampire blood and becomes a half vampire, like Star.

Unlike the boys' mother, who is focused on trying to begin her new life, their grandfather is well aware of what's going on. He says nothing to interfere, but keeps calm and stays on the periphery, paying close attention and sharing obscure folklore and facts. Until he's needed: that's when he swoops in to save the day. (And utters one of the great final lines in modern cinema: "One thing about living in Santa Carla I never could stomach: all the damn vampires.")

We, too, can practice informed awareness—though unlike Grandpa, it's best if we let our kids know that our eyes are open and we'll be there if they need us. Maybe there's no vampire gang to worry about, but unfortunately kids' social circles are vulnerable to real-life dangers like addiction, cyberbullying, and sexual abuse. Our awareness not only allows us to monitor for red flags, it sends our children the message that we care and are paying attention. If an emergency comes up, we stand ready to drive antlers through the heart of the head vampire— or do whatever the situation calls for to keep our kids out of harm's way.

Leonardo, Donatello, Raphael, Michelangelo, and Splinter teach us:

CHOOSE YOUR BATTLES WISELY, AS A NINJA SHOULD.

When a super-intelligent mutant rat named Splinter finds four mutated baby turtles, he takes them in and raises them as his sons, teaching them martial arts so that they can protect themselves. Splinter gives them the names of his favorite Renaissance artists—Leonardo, Donatello, Raphael, and Michelangelo—and he tries to instruct them to live a well-balanced life. Much as their four namesakes mastered a host of different skills, each of the Teenage Mutant Ninja Turtles has particular strengths and weaknesses. As their sensei as well as their adoptive father, Splinter trains the Turtles with their weapons of choice: Leonardo wields two katanas, Donatello has a *bō* staff, Raphael fights with a pair of sais, and Michelangelo uses a pair of nunchaku. But even more valuable is the wisdom Splinter offers to temper their use of physical force. A skilled warrior, the rat guru does not encourage his sons to fight needlessly. As he tells Raphael in the 1990 *TMNT* movie: "My Master Yoshi's first rule was, 'Possess the right thinking. Only then can one receive the gifts of strength, knowledge, and peace.'"

There are myriad ways to defend oneself; both personal ideology and available resources will impact which methods parents will choose to teach to their children. For Master Splinter, it means teaching his sons the ninja arts. For some parents, it may be training their kids in the finer points of debate and rhetoric, or simply instilling in them the courage of their convictions. The important thing is that we not only equip our children with tools they can use to feel confident but also help them understand how and when to use them.

For all the battles they fight, the Teenage Mutant Ninja Turtles often show us that a large part of self-defense has nothing to do with combat training. It involves other skills, like self-confidence, awareness of one's surroundings, attracting other people's attention, trusting one's intuition, and choosing to walk away before a situation escalates. From Master Splinter and his turtacular boys, we learn that knowing how to fight is valuable, but so is the wisdom of knowing when not to.

Perseus and Zeus teach us:

BE CAREFUL HOW AND WHEN YOU RELEASE THE KRAKEN.

The 1981 film *Clash of the Titans* brought the ancient Greek gods and heroes to life on the movie screen. Taking some liberties from the original myths, the film revolves around the life of the demigod Perseus, son of Danaë of Argos and Zeus, king of the gods. Seeking to prevent a prophecy of his destruction at the hands of his grandson, King Acrisius of Argos orders Perseus and his mother to be sealed in a wooden crate and cast into the sea. But Zeus protects them, and they're carried safely to a nearby island. In retribution for the king's crime, Zeus orders Poseidon to release the Kraken, an enormous sea creature, to wreak havoc on Acrisius's realm.

Generally understood to mean unleashing one's wrath upon an adversary, "Release the Kraken!" became a well-known catchphrase in the movie's wake. Then, three decades later, it gained renewed notoriety with the 2010 remake of *Clash of the Titans*, popping up across the Internet in memes and videos that often poked fun at Liam Neeson's delivery. It was Laurence Olivier who made the line famous in the original film, capturing the emotion of an enraged father looking to destroy the man who attempted to have his son killed.

When someone tries to hurt our children, we often discover within ourselves a protective and vengeful streak that would rival the intensity of gods in any pantheon. We would do almost anything to keep our children safe, and that's a good thing—except when it's misdirected. Zeus releases the Kraken to punish Acrisius for trying to kill Perseus and his mother, but in unleashing the beast, he destroys the entire kingdom of Argos.

If a child we love is injured or wronged and someone else is at fault, releasing our metaphorical Kraken in response may be a natural reaction. The challenge is figuring out how to temper or modify our outrage. At times, we need to allow kids to fight their own battles; at other times, they need us to be their advocates. And then there are the exceptional times, when we encounter an instance of profound wrongdoing against a child, and we need to pour our intense emotion into rallying the larger community to work toward justice.

Adults are supposed to do everything possible to help make the world safer and better for our children—all of them. We may be called to respond in provocative and powerful ways, putting ourselves on the front lines of collective action. In other words, sometimes releasing the Kraken is exactly what's called for.

A LIFE OF RUM AND FAST SHIPS SEEMS LIKE A REAL BLAST, TILL YOU FIND YOURSELF IMPRISONED BENEATH THE WAVES FOR ALL ETERNITY.

To watch Jack Sparrow is a lot of fun. Sword in hand, he swashbuckles to match the greatest pirate captains in history. He's clever of tongue, always ready with the witty phrase we wish we would have thought of. And he's sexy as hell. In contrast to that romantic image, Jack likes his rum a little too much. Well, no, let's not be polite. Jack Sparrow is a raging alcoholic, to the point where the Urban Dictionary defines the phrase "Jack Sparrow Drunk" as "drinking alcohol nonstop, never sobering up, and still accomplishing things most people can't manage to do sober."

It sounds glamorous when you put it that way. And, indeed, the *Pirates of the Caribbean* franchise finally gave us the perfect justification for that depiction: Captain Jack's dad is Keith Richards. In the most metatextually on-the-nose casting coup ever, elder pirate statesman Captain Teague is played by the rock star most singularly famous worldwide for drinking all the booze, doing all the drugs, and still

being one of the greatest guitarists rock and roll has ever seen. Jack Sparrow, like that classic '80s drug-awareness commercial, can fairly say: "Dad, I learned it from watching you."

Growing up with an addict as a parent doesn't mean that a child is sure to become one. But statistically it does increase the odds. That's not just genetics; it's also the effect of having internalized the parent's behavior as normal. Nevertheless, forewarned is forearmed. The generational cycle of addictive behavior can be broken. One good starting point: realizing that whatever dysfunctional coping mechanisms we inherit from our parents don't *have* to be passed on to our children.

Jack Sparrow's philosophy on dealing with life's challenges— "Close your eyes and pretend it's all a bad dream. That's how I get by"—works only until, suddenly, it doesn't. Here's a vastly more useful approach: we can confront our afflictions head-on, admit to them, seek help, and be honest about our struggle for recovery. Ultimately, that kind of openness, rather than a bunch of rock-star anecdotes about a parent's destructive exploits, will give our children more stable sea legs.

Scott Summers, Jean Grey, Rachel, and Cable teach us:

YOU CAN'T CHANGE YOUR FAMILY'S PAST—ONLY HURTLE BOLDLY WITH THEM INTO THE FUTURE.

s there a crazier sci-fi soap opera in all of comics than the Summers bunch? After Scott's fiancée Jean sacrificed her life to save the X-Men (and the whole world) from being destroyed by her omnipotent Phoenix powers, Rachel—their future daughter from an alternate timeline—taps into those same powers to travel back in time. She wants to make everything better, only to discover that Scott married a mysterious doppelganger of Jean named Madelyn Pryor, who turns out to be an evil clone . . . and gives birth to Scott's infant son Nathan . . . who is kidnapped and infected with a deadly techno-organic virus. In order to save Nathan, yet another time traveler takes the baby into an even farther-off future than Rachel's, where the disease can be stopped. Nathan grows up to be a middle-aged man called Cable, and unaware of his true identity, eventually he, too, travels back in time and joins a different group of X-Men before finally coming into conflict with Scott. Jean, by the way, has come back from the grave. And we haven't even mentioned how Scott's father, whom Scott always thought was long dead, has in fact just been kidnapped by aliens and turned into a space pirate. So, yeah, this family's backstory is real messed up.

Then again, isn't yours? Isn't everybody's? We all dream

wistfully of being able to undo, to redo, the moments when our family history ran off the rails. When a child suffered a traumatic experience, when a beloved cousin fell prey to addiction, when a grandparent's die-hard homophobia caused a rift that severed branches of relations from others. But, unlike the X-Men's chronologically complicated Summers family, we don't have time travel as an option. It's all too easy to waste precious time and energy beating ourselves up over things gone wrong, things we blame ourselves for, things we're sure we'd do differently if we could just go back. That's understandable, but not particularly helpful. (Besides, even with time travel, the Summers clan is a mess.)

Faced with our broken world, we have to accept today's reality, even if our family's lives may have turned out differently than we'd hoped. The good news is that we *can* change things for the better—not by obsessively revisiting the past, but by traveling forward into the future, one day at a time.

5

CHANGE IS THE ESSENTIAL PROCESS OF ALL EXISTENCE *

Helping them grow and evolve into advanced beings.

THE NAME YOU GIVE THEM MAY NOT BE THE NAME THEY CHOOSE.

We devote a lot of thought to choosing the names of our children. Should it be a family name to connect the child with a loved one? Or words with a specific meaning that will guide our children as their personalities develop? It's a decision we pour plenty of sweat into, and understandably so: a name is more than just what a parent yells out the window to make sure the right kid comes home for dinner. Names hold intention; they are tied to baby blessings and coming-of-age ceremonies, bestowed upon children in sacred rituals of cultures around the world. Among the Yoruba of Nigeria, for example, children are given "destiny names" for special circumstances around their birth. Ashkenazi Jews often name babies after deceased loved ones. Names carry a lot of weight—from parents, family, and community.

In Octavia Butler's postapocalyptic 1998 novel *Parable of the Talents*, the heroine's name—Larkin Beryl Ife Olamina Bankole—is carefully constructed to connect her with her ancestry and heritage. Part of her name comes from her famous mother, Lauren Oya Olamina, founder of the Earthseed religion, who passes up the chance to move her family to safety after hearing about threats from warring factions. It's a fateful decision: young Larkin ends up being kidnapped by the invaders and adopted by Christian American parents, who rename her Asha Vere. After a difficult life apart, daughter and mother are eventually reunited. But when Olamina calls Larkin by her original name, the younger woman rejects it, claiming instead the one given by her foster parents. Asha no longer cares to bear the connections and connotations associated with her given name.

Fairy-tale wisdom says that to know someone's true name is to have power over that person. Names do have power, and choosing one's own is an exercise in autonomy—an act of asserting one's self over the world's preconceptions. Like Asha who once was Larkin, our children may someday claim a new name that better reflects the way they see themselves.

Even without the backstory of Lauren and Larkin, it can be hard to accept when our precious Sarah or Justin wants to be called Starfire or Money J. But is it such a crime that the name you picked, probably before you even laid eyes on your child, turns out to not quite fit? The truth is, when we look upon our babies, we have no idea who they will grow into. We meet them anew again and again, throughout their lives. Hopefully, we're simply happy to meet them each time, whatever they want to be called.

Bruce Wayne and Alfred Pennyworth teach us:

IF YOUR CHILD IS CALLED TO BE THE HERO GOTHAM DESERVES—THAT'S HER CALL TO MAKE.

lfred Pennyworth served as butler to the Waynes of Gotham long enough that he became one of the family. All the more literally and tragically so when his employers, Thomas and Martha Wayne, were murdered, leaving their young son Bruce to be raised in Alfred's care. So it's hard to blame Alfred for being less than enthusiastic about Bruce's decision to spend his life dressing up in a bat costume to attack the most violently insane criminals he can find. "I've buried enough members of the Wayne family," Alfred pleads with Bruce in 2012's *The Dark Knight Rises.* "I wanted something more for you than that."

To feel that you've been uniquely called to a higher purpose is a special thing. But though most kids aren't destined to be Batman, Bruce Wayne was hardly the first strong-willed youngster to set his resolve upon attaining a difficult achievement that would require years of sacrifice with no guarantee of success. We see it when a grade-schooler excels at gymnastics and makes up

his mind he'll someday win a gold medal. We see it when a blossoming young adult decides to go into a thankless or perilous line of work—soldier, firefighter—because she wants to make the world a better place. And we see it when a disadvantaged child decides to be the first in the family to graduate from college, never mind the economic challenges or obstacles arrayed ahead.

The parenting danger here is twofold, and it looms simultaneously from opposite directions. On the one hand, we want to resist the urge to push our kids to achieve the accolades we always wanted for ourselves—to shape their lives (as a few too many football dads and dance moms have done over the years) for our own vicarious excitement. On the other hand, when our child tells us that he or she is prepared to give up all that free after-school playtime, all those wide-open summers, in order to train like crazy for a shot at someday making the Olympic team—well, that kind of commitment from one so young is rare, and it's worth honoring.

Who knows? Someday, your kid's face, name, or jersey number might be the inspiration that younger children wear on their T-shirts. Just like Batman.

Paul Atreides and Lady Jessica teach us:

YOU CAN CHART A MASTER PLAN FOR YOUR FAMILY'S LIFE, BUT ONE GIANT SANDWORM CAN KNOCK EVERYTHING OFF COURSE.

ady Jessica had a grand scheme all laid out. She would perfect the skills and talents taught to her as a member of the secret Bene Gesserit Sisterhood. She would partner and mate with Duke Leto Atreides. She would give birth to his daughter. That daughter would marry the Baron Harkonnen's young nephew, Feyd-Rautha. And eventually that couple would give birth to a son to fulfill the promise of the Bene Gesserit's carefully mapped-out breeding program and produce a more highly evolved humanity.

Things don't work out that way. First, Jessica takes a left

turn from the plan because she thinks she can speed up the Bene Gesserit time frame *and* make her beloved Duke happy by producing a male heir a generation early. After that, it all goes kerflooey. The emperor surprises the Atreides clan by sending them to the desert planet Arrakis. Then a perfect storm of cutthroat politics, unpredictable catastrophes, and terrifying giant sandworms the size of starships leaves Leto dead, Jessica and her son Paul fugitives on the run, and the whole Bene Gesserit master plan more or less in shambles. At which point Jessica's goals become much more straightforward: keep my son alive.

Plans (or in the case of Frank Herbert's *Dune* novels, "Plans within plans within plans") are good. They bring intention to our lives, and that's no small matter. The hitch is when we mistake intention for control—when we forget that the map we're drawing for ourselves isn't a program that the whole universe must follow. And when kids are involved, anything from an unexpected case of the sniffles to a decision to change majors (or drop out) can upend your blueprint for the day, the year, or the foreseeable future.

The solution isn't to stop planning, but to be willing to scrap a scheme when it becomes untenable and then improvise a new one. Who knows? Maybe, just maybe, the sandworm that crushed your ornithopter could become your ticket out of the desert.

DON'T THREATEN YOUR MAGIC PRINCESS'S SUITORS. BUT DO HELP HER UNDERSTAND WHAT IT MEANS TO LOVE A MORTAL.

Dating is one of those milestones that parents dread precisely because we have so little control over it. Most of us can remember the way reason takes a backseat to the powerful emotions that overwhelm us in the early stages of love. For young lovers, nothing else matters except being together. Unfortunately, age and experience teach us there's a lot more to be considered.

In J. R. R. Tolkien's Lord of the Rings saga, Arwen, a half-Elf maiden, falls in love with Aragorn, of the race of Men. She is immortal and, in fact, nearly 2,700 years his senior. If Arwen chooses to remain in Middle-earth with her love, rather than travel with the rest of the Elves to the Blessed Realms, she will eventually have to watch Aragorn die. Arwen's father, Elrond, doesn't want to leave his daughter behind when he sails west; he's already lost his twin brother to a similar choice. But while he desperately wants to prevent his daughter's inevitable heartache, the choice isn't his to make. Elrond must accept that his daughter chooses a shorter life with her beloved, rather than immortality without him.

Every relationship that children enter into brings its own set of challenges. What we can do is provide our kids with a big-picture view of what intimacy entails—and of the spectrum of consequences they may face. Like Arwen, our sons and daughters may date someone of a different race or religion or culture; if they do, they may have to deal with societal prejudices. If they choose to have sex, they need to understand the way intimacy can change the dynamic of a relationship, and that it can alter their entire lives if they don't use protection. If they decide to live together, married or otherwise, they will have to figure out the logistics of individuals merging personal effects, routines, and finances.

Our children may feel certain that no one in the history of the universe has ever felt the way they feel—that theirs is a magical love that will last forever. (Remember what that felt like?) Maybe their love will weather the trials of growing up and figuring out one's identity; maybe it won't. But as tempting as it sometimes is to step in and take charge in order to spare them from heartbreak, assuming that responsibility is not the way to a happy ending. Kids need to find their own version of happily ever after. Meanwhile, we should stand ready to hug and advise them through a lot of dating, heartache, and healing along the way.

Marty, Lorraine, and George McFly teach us:

LEARNING THAT ONE'S PARENTS USED TO BE DORKY KIDS IS A POWERFUL CONFIDENCE BOOST— AT LEAST 1.21 GIGAWATTS WORTH.

Kids have a hard time grasping that their parents were once awkward teenagers. That we, like them, lived through some combination of glasses, braces, acne, terrible fashion sense, and bad haircuts. When they first look at our old photos, they may not recognize Mom's big hair or Dad's mullet. But they'd probably identify with the emotional angst many of us felt as we tried to fit in, to avoid getting the wrong kind of attention, to figure out who we wanted to be. Being a teenager is not easy today, nor was it easy in the 1990s or the 1950s or any era you can imagine.

In *Back to the Future*, Marty McFly time-travels from 1984 to 1955 in Doc Brown's DeLorean and meets George, his dorky teenage father. The film's plot picks up speed when Marty accidentally interrupts the moment when his parents are supposed to meet. The result: an alternate future where George and Lorraine never marry and Marty and his siblings are never born. The film is mostly concerned with Marty's frantic efforts to reinstate his own existence. But Marty also gains a rare opportunity to see his father at his vulnerable, nerdy worst, and they become friends.

Kids often see adults as people who have all the answers. They don't know that many of us sometimes still feel the same on the inside as we did when we were younger. There may be something gained from showing our kids the teenagers we once were. Though we can't go back in time, we can share stories and photographs. Indeed, the advent of social media memes like Throwback Thursday has made it easier than ever to embrace our dorky childhood selves. With those embarrassing photos from school plays and dances, academic decathlons and science fairs, we can show our kids that we got past the stress of grades, school power dynamics, and clique politics. We (mostly) outgrew our dorky looks and questionable style choices, and we survived feeling sad and alone. Seeing that we did it should give our kids hope that they can, too.

Scott and Harold Howard teach us:

TEENAGERS ARE BASICALLY WEREWOLVES. THEIR BODIES ARE ALWAYS CHANGING.

There's nothing supernatural about it: teenage boys essentially lose control of their bodies and emotions and go through a series of transformations. Their frames grow, their voices change, hair sprouts up in unfamiliar places—and then all those urges arise. It's not a big leap from the reality of puberty to the allegory of the werewolf.

Your typical 1980s teenager, the *Teen Wolf* protagonist Scott Howard is trying to survive high school, carve out a name for himself, and get the attention of the pretty Pamela. "I'm sick of being so average," he tells Boof, his best friend from childhood. Then strange things begin to happen to his body. Scott locks himself in the bathroom at home, watching in horror at the metamorphosis in the mirror.

From *I Was a Teenage Werewolf* to *The Lost Boys* to *Twilight*, there's no shortage of films and books that view puberty and adolescence through a paranormal lens. Add lycanthropy or vampirism to the Petri dish of teenage angst and hormones, and the result is horror or comedy (or both). Different monsters face difference challenges, but all these films ask the question that teenagers everywhere are wondering: *How can I get power when I feel so powerless?*

Scott learns that he has inherited the werewolf condition

from his father, Harold, who reassures him that what's happening isn't all that unusual or terrible. "The werewolf is a part of you," Harold tells his son, "but that doesn't change what you have inside." This message is the heart of the film, and it's what we can impart to our children when they're in the midst of crazy changes. Whether they're awkward cranky misfits or shiny too-cool all-stars, our teenagers are still the same kids we raised. They're just trying to figure out how they fit into a world where they have so little control over anything, even their own bodies.

Pamela's boyfriend Mick taunts Scott, saying, "Underneath all that hair, you're still a dork." Mick intends his statement to be a dig, as if the teenager is somehow less than the werewolf. But in fact it echoes the advice of Scott's father. Maybe Scott is a dork under all that hair—and that's okay. He has teammates who respect him, friends who love him, and a dad who supports him. The teen half of Teen Wolf is already pretty great. That's the answer to the question of where teens get their power: they've had it all along. Kids need to know that we love the person inside no matter what the person outside looks like. We hope that, eventually, they'll figure out the inside is the part that really counts.

Sarah Manning and Mrs. S. teach us:

NO ONE WANTS TO LOOK LIKE JUST ANOTHER CLONE.

Expressing one's individuality is important, especially when you're a clone. The BBC America series *Orphan Black* focuses on the converging lives of several clones who team up to uncover their past and save their sisters. Early on in the show, someone asks one of the clones, Sarah Manning, if there are nine of her. She replies, "No, there's only one of me." And it's true: their identical genes notwithstanding, each of the clones played by Tatiana Maslany is a unique and well-rounded character, even when one of them dons another's clothes and pretends to be her.

Taken in by Siobhan "Mrs. S." Sadler, Sarah and her foster brother Felix are raised on the run, moving from the U.K. to Canada one step ahead of the scientists and fanatics who'd like to get their hands on Sarah to study her unique physiology. Even as she devotes her life to keeping Sarah safe, Mrs. S. allows Sarah the space to make her own choices and grow into a savvy, street-smart survivor.

Kids have a lot to figure out as they try on different personalities and styles, sorting out what the media is pushing, what their friends want, what they think their parents expect, and what they themselves really like. Finding a balance between all those voices is where we can help, by listening, as Mrs. S. does, without judgment and by supporting them when they try new things. If we want our children to develop a strong sense of self, it's important to encourage their healthy expressions of individuality. Especially amid a culture that broadcasts some strong messages about conformity and what are and aren't acceptable standards of beauty.

Our children may choose hippie chic or gender-bending glam or straight-up preppy or something that's not even named yet—maybe all in one week. They may decide to mismatch their clothes, wear the same color every day, or choose a hairstyle that we don't particularly like. It's not about us, what we like or want. It's about our kids having the courage and support to figure out what sort of imprint they want to leave as they move through the world.

Virgil, Robert, and Sharon Hawkins teach us:

NOT EVERY KID MAKES THE VARSITY TEAM RIGHT OUT OF THE GATE. BUT YOU NEVER KNOW WHEN LIGHTNING MIGHT STRIKE.

Sometimes the lesson we learn from a geek tale doesn't come from the text, but from the behind-the-scenes true story of its creators. Take Static, the electromagnetically powered teen hero who originated as one of the lead characters of the Milestone Comics universe, an African American–founded superhero line that published as an independent imprint of DC Comics. In his secret identity as Virgil Hawkins, Static learns from his parents and older sister—all healthcare professionals—the value and the difficulty of making a positive impact on the world.

Unfortunately, Milestone produced comic books for only four years before shutting down. But something unexpected, yet well-deserved, happened. Warner Bros. Animation, in need of a new hit show to build on its *Batman* and *Superman* successes, bypassed every other DC hero, from Wonder Woman to Green Lantern, and tapped Static. The *Static Shock* cartoon ran for four seasons, winning accolades and nominations for several television awards.

The comic book marketplace might not have supported Static, but TV sure did. We see that sort of phenomenon unfold in childhood life, too. Not everyone will recognize and respect the worth of any given kid. But some people will, and the love and energy in those connections can make all the difference, generating the necessary fortitude to keep on slugging through life's hard days and on to better times.

The lessons Static learns from his family align with what we glean from watching the character's rise to prominence. No matter how many obstacles the world piles in front of you, stay true to yourself and keep striving. It's the only way to make it to the big leagues.

CHILDREN OF TWO WORLDS OFTEN FEEL THEY BELONG TO NEITHER.

When his mother K'Ehleyr is killed, young Alexander joins his father, Lieutenant Worf, on the USS *Enterprise*. Worf quickly sends the boy to Earth to be raised by his adoptive parents, the Rozhenkos, preferring his son to have a human upbringing rather than a Klingon one. Alexander, one-quarter human and three-quarters Klingon, is uncertain where he fits in; he has trouble adjusting to life on Earth and is eventually returned to the *Enterprise* to live with Worf. There, the boy still feels out of place, for he has a hard time getting the hang of life aboard a starship. He befriends Counselor Deanna Troi and her mother, Lwaxana, who try to help him enjoy his new home. But Alexander continues to struggle with his identity and his relationship with his father.

Here at the dawn of the twenty-first century, the old-fashioned scenario of two folks from the same small town falling in love as high school sweethearts is being replaced by so many other possibilities. In

the increasingly global culture that younger generations are inheriting, individuals from different nations and ideologies come together in romantic relationships that were less likely in previous decades. Even if our own children are not raised in a household that blends two rich, disparate cultural heritages, there's a good chance they'll make friends with kids who are. And like Alexander, youngsters in that situation may grow up feeling like they belong in neither world.

If we look to the *Star Trek* universe, we find it's often the characters who live on the threshold who are most beloved by fans. Spock, Data, Odo, Worf—with one foot in each world, they view things as an outsider. They teach us that in trying to balance the two sides of one's nature, it is the ability to move between diverse worlds that's the greatest gift.

Kids in that situation are sometimes pulled in multiple directions. Which is when we should remind them that home is ultimately the place filled with people we love—those individuals we name as our family, regardless of race, religion, or planet of origin.

Rose and Jackie Tyler teach us:

THERE'S NO SUCH THING AS BEING "JUST A SHOP GIRL."

When we first meet *Doctor Who*'s Rose Tyler, she's working in a department store. She doesn't hate it, nor does she seem terribly distracted by dreams of something bigger. She's got a boyfriend whom she finds amusing; she makes enough money so she's not just mooching off her mother, Jackie. And in the brief moments we glimpse of her mundane workaday life, Rose seems confident that she's one of the most competent people in her world. She's a blue-collar kid with a "sensible" view of life, satisfied with young adulthood, and not especially driven to go to university or pursue any particular ambition. She's, you know, "average."

But that's before she meets the Doctor. That's before she's given the chance to consider the vastness of the cosmos and the infinite possibilities that wait unrealized in the future. Confronted with just how much larger the universe is than she'd ever considered, Rose barely hesitates before leaping into the time-and-space machine that offers her so much more. And as she spends long months traveling with a Time Lord, one thing becomes certain: whether or not she stays with him forever, she'll never return to the life she had before. She can't—because she's not that person anymore. And Jackie, though she doesn't understand why, is quick to see how her daughter has changed.

Rose Tyler isn't an honors student. Her single mom isn't well-off. She lives in the decaying inner city and speaks with a working-class accent. She grew up with certain expectations about what her life would look like. And you know what? Anyone who would judge her worth as a person by those facts is an ass. Given the chance, given the experience, Rose Tyler helped save the world—again and again. So if your family's not fancy, make sure your kids understand that a person's birth circumstance isn't destiny. And if your family *is* fancy, make sure they understand the exact same thing.

Princess Diana and Queen Hippolyta teach us:

IT'S HARD TO JUGGLE YOUR KINGDOM AND YOUR KIDS, ESPECIALLY WHEN YOUR DAUGHTER WANTS TO SAVE THE WORLD.

One of the few prominent mothers in superhero comics, Queen Hippolyta of the Amazons often feels torn between her responsibilities as mother to the high-achieving Princess Diana and her full-time job as ruler of a secret island civilization. It's a familiar source of tension. How do we maintain balance and sanity when trying to reconcile our children's needs with our own? For three millennia, Hippolyta presides peacefully over Paradise Island. She tries her hardest to control her daughter's actions when she senses Diana's curiosity about Man's World. But when the time comes to send a champion as emissary to the United States, Princess Diana is victorious in the competition among the Amazons. Despite Hippolyta's strong objections, she must fulfill her royal obligation and send her daughter to join humanity as Wonder Woman.

The thing about balance is that we constantly have to adjust if we want to maintain it. When our children are little, we do whatever we can to keep them safe. Then comes a point when they challenge our authority. Our role changes as they grow, and we need to continue recalibrating. Through it all we need to expend time and energy on our other responsibilities, whether managing a household, navigating a career, or running an island nation.

The 3,000-year-old Hippolyta still makes mistakes. She falls into the trap of becoming overly involved in her daughter's life—even, at one point, taking the role of Wonder Woman for herself. But Diana routinely defeats armies and villains; she faces down death and divinity. She has grown up. She no longer needs Hippolyta the way she once did.

It's possible to get so wrapped up in the juggling of home and work that, when the kids no longer need us, we're again thrown off balance. Hippolyta deals with her own version of empty-nest syndrome: when Diana leaves for the outside world, the queen is left to figure out what remains of her authentic self. Like Wonder Woman's mom, we must keep reenvisioning ourselves, so that when our kids move on to jobs and families of their own, we're not only proud of who they are but also happy with ourselves.

AT SOME POINT, YOU WILL DECLARE YOUR CHILD TO BE A MONSTER OF EVIL.

We all have moments when the shoes that fit our child yesterday don't fit today, when the spaghetti is too hard to eat, when the homework is impossible to do, when the temperature is too hot and the night is too dark and the siblings are too annoying. It all comes to a head with tears and shouting and meltdowns, and somebody ends up in the corner, either hiding or pouting or rocking or all three at once. These are the apocalypse days of parenting, and though (thankfully) they don't happen all the time, they do happen.

In the "Stewie Loves Lois" episode of the animated TV show *Family Guy*, we see Lois lying in bed, staring bleary-eyed as her megalomaniacal infant son repeats again and again: "Lois, Mom, Mommy, Mama, Ma, Mum" for thirty-five seconds straight, until finally she turns to him and snaps, "What?" To which he replies, "Hi," and runs away giggling.

That moment, admittedly one of the more innocent examples to be found on the satirical animated sitcom, illustrates the taunting and torture that can be a part of parenthood. We may wonder if, like Stewie, our children are hell-bent on destruction. More specifically, *our* destruction.

Baby Stewie may focus on diabolical plots to take over the world, but he's still a baby. He lacks the common sense and cultural context that come with age and experience. In a show full of irreverent associative acrobatics, much of what we find funny about Stewie comes from his misperceptions of the world and his witty observations about his dysfunctional family.

Our children are probably not criminal masterminds, but they are definitely capable of acting like terrors. Parenting isn't all cheerful family game nights and cozy bedtime stories. There will be moments of sibling warfare and manipulative mind games that would stress out even the wisest of Jedi masters. Sometimes our darling angels can be the grumpiest of monsters, and we wish we could send them to their own Fortress of Solitude or Pandorica—at least for a few minutes of peace and quiet.

So when we're at the TSA checkpoint and the alarms go off calling security, all because our child's backpack contains a porcupine made of Play-Doh and pipe cleaners that looks just like a bomb on the X-ray scanner . . . on days like that, there's not much else to do but know that every parent has been there. Just start counting down the minutes until bedtime. You will live to parent another day.

Sherlock Holmes and his parents teach us:

IT'S ELEMENTARY. SOMETIMES THE APPLE FALLS FAR FROM THE TREE.

When our children are born, we see in their faces hints of ourselves. Do they have their grandfather's chin or mom's eyes? Their brother's hair or an aunt's cheekbones? We watch and wonder about what else they've inherited. But what happens if they share none of our own skills or interests? How do we parent children who seem to be nothing like us?

As played by Benedict Cumberbatch in the BBC's 2010s adaptation of Sir Arthur Conan Doyle's detective series, Sherlock Holmes is a genius whose arrogant stoicism sets him apart. "Love is an emotional thing," says Sherlock, "and whatever is emotional is opposed to that true cold reason which I place above all things."

That is why audiences are surprised when they glimpse his family at the end of season three. For a man defined by his detachment and self-imposed alienation, Sherlock's parents are inexplicably caring and interested and . . . normal.

Genetics and upbringing are no guarantee that children will be in any way like their parents. That's challenging, but it's also okay. Sherlock's parents don't have to be his intellectual friends. They just have to let him know that their differences are far less important than the bond they share.

CATS MAY HAVE NINE LIVES, BUT WE GET ONLY ONE. SO LIVE EACH DAY WITH PURPOSE.

'Chaka, the late ruler of Marvel Comics' fictional African nation of Wakanda, was as noble and parental a monarch as they come. His land was the only source of the all-but-indestructible metal called vibranium. T'Chaka worked hard to protect his people from exploitation and the violence that would surely follow if the metal's presence became known. He then raised his son T'Challa to understand his philosophies of peace and security.

Alas, the tranquil reign does not last. An assassin murders the king, leaving young T'Challa to take up the hereditary warrior title of Black Panther. As both ruler and a member of the Avengers, T'Challa does his father proud. Given the choice, he'd certainly wish T'Chaka were still alive. But fortunately the old king took the time to teach the lessons that mattered most.

Such is the reality of a human life: we don't get to choose, or know, our expiration date. If we're lucky, we have loving parents who see us well into our adulthood, and then we do the same for our kids. But there's no guarantee that our story won't be cut short before we're ready. It's a reason to love our children, and tell them so, every day. And to show by example what it means to live a purposeful life.

Claudia, Louis, and Lestat teach us:

WE CAN'T KEEP THEM LITTLE FOREVER.

These days, vampires and family drama go hand-in-hand. But it wasn't really until Anne Rice introduced the world to Lestat, Louis, and Claudia in her 1976 novel *Interview with the Vampire* that we began to see the dynamics of carefully constructed vampire families in fiction. Lestat and Louis become "parents" to the five-year-old Claudia after Lestat turns her undead in hopes it will shore up the pair's relationship. As they eventually discover, using a child as an emotional bandage never really fixes anything. Although the immortal family is happy enough for the first sixty-five years, their problems don't go away. And Claudia grows increasingly resentful of her two fathers for having trapped her in a little girl's body that can never mature.

Sometimes parents muse that if their children could just stay little forever, they could keep them close and safe. We typically think of separation anxiety as something that children experience, but parents feel it, too. When kids go off to school, to camp, to college—whenever a child puts time and space between us, we feel the temptation to hold on tighter lest they slip too far away. Sometimes we do this literally: hugging them close, keeping them nearby, limiting their involvement with others. Sometimes we use constant communication to tether them to us with calls, texts, and emails. But kids need time and space to pull away so that they can figure out who they are. It's part of their development to question our judgment and ideals and see themselves as separate from the people who raised them.

Claudia never really has the chance to develop beyond a five-year-old level of self-centered emotional intensity. Where Louis deals with vampirism by fiercely clutching onto his human side, Claudia evolves into a sadistic predator in the body of a beautiful child. Louis remains protective of his daughter, but she resents her eternal dependence. She can never sire another vampire, nor experience so many joys of being a grown woman. Claudia will never really be able to break away from her "parents," and she will never have the chance to find her way back to them on her own terms.

Growing up requires children to experience the full spectrum of human experience for themselves, from joy to heartache. If we try to keep them trapped in our expectations, we are far more likely to lose them.

Kara "Starbuck" Thrace and William Adama teach us:

FORGIVE THEM. ALL THIS HAS HAPPENED BEFORE, AND ALL THIS WILL HAPPEN AGAIN.

From the time they're little, some kids challenge all the rules. They disdain convention, reject opinions, and learn their lesson only after burning their hand on the stove. It's easy to imagine the impetuous Kara "Starbuck" Thrace as just such a child. The Colonial fleet's best Viper pilot in the reenvisioned *Battlestar Galactica* TV series, she breaks orders, takes risks, and spits in the face of authority at every turn.

Engaged to Commander Adama's son Zak, who dies before they marry, Starbuck is treated by Adama like the daughter she could have been. The commander admires her skill and encourages her to take a leadership role while also trying to teach her to temper her impertinence. It's a familiar dynamic, one often depicted in 1950s TV shows like *Ozzy and Harriet*: a kid makes a mistake, then has a long talk with Dad to figure out the error of their ways, and all is forgiven. In *Battlestar Galactica,* where Adama is the central authority figure for the weary hordes of the dwindling human race, that pattern plays out again and again, especially for Starbuck.

The show is *Father Knows Best* with killer robots in outer space. At a time when everything is in flux and no one knows what they can hold on to or believe in, Adama's integrity is unquestionable and his support unwavering. Watching

Starbuck commandeer Vipers and flip off her superiors and Cylons, we worry about her safety. But we know that Adama will forgive her. Because *BSG* is a show about forgiving mistakes once deemed unforgivable. And Commander Adama is the forgiver-in-chief at the head (and heart) of it all.

That makes a pretty good job description for a parent. It's hard to stay calm when reading yet another note from the teacher about some grievance or misdemeanor. But getting angry takes the spotlight off the real issue: our child made a bad choice. Why? What are the consequences? What can he or she learn from the experience? Adama reminds us that parenting is not about our ego; it's about doing what's best for the people in our care. Forgiveness allows us to let go of anger and hold on to what really matters—our child. Adama could have embraced his righteous rage when Starbuck defied him. But he didn't, and that's what makes him a good role model.

"You cannot play God and then wash your hands of the things that you've created," Adama says early in the series. Rather, you've got to hang in there, figure out what went wrong, and work toward redemption. Adama was talking about the killer robots, but he was also talking about his kids . . . and ours, too.

INDEX